D0354064

MY
FAVORITE
INGREDIENTS

◊

PHOTOGRAPHY BY
Jason Lowe

TEN SPEED PRESS
Berkeley

SKYE GYNGELL

WITHDRAWN

My *favorite* ingredients

An enticing *collection* of recipes

Please use sea salt, freshly ground pepper, and fresh herbs (except in the rare instances where I have specified dried herbs).

I use medium organic eggs. Anyone who is pregnant or in a vulnerable health group should avoid recipes using raw egg whites or lightly cooked eggs.

Introduction

More than anything else, I would describe my cooking as produce driven. At Petersham Nurseries Café, we compose our menus daily—when the fresh produce arrives and we know for certain what is available and at its best. It is when I see the beautiful cream and crimson fleck of the first Castelfranco of the year, for example, that I begin to consider what it would work with—perhaps succulent fresh crab or the sweet bitter flavor of blood oranges, or maybe young romano or oven-roasted squab. It might be the particular color of an olive oil or the sweet intensity of a type of vinegar that gives a certain dish its real character for me. Beautiful ingredients will take a dish to new heights. At the restaurant, we follow the seasons closely. I believe that food eaten in its right season and grown as close to home as possible tastes far better than food flown in from afar. I also believe that nature provides ingredients in the same season that go together perfectly. Pairing seasonal produce is where I have the most fun in the kitchen.

I express myself through the way I cook. Food truly captures my heart, and the kitchen is where I feel confident and at home. Nowhere else do I feel so free, or so connected at the same time. Food fascinates, seduces, and entrances me. Produce in its purest form, in peak condition—tasting as it should—can lift and dazzle me with the excitement of its possibilities.

My knowledge of produce—its history, place, variety, and season, as well as learning how to prepare and use it—has come to me gradually over the years and I'm still on a voyage of discovery. I continue, for example, to learn about the varieties and nuances of flavor of all the different honeys. Year in, year out, I come across a different variety of bean or salad leaf that I fall in love with and wonder how it was possible to cook without it.

Seeking out good produce has introduced me to many local suppliers and farmers over the years—we currently work with no less than 47 different providers. These people are important to me, and my relationships with them have developed over time. They are experts on their particular produce and I learn so much from them. I'm fortunate to work in an industry where people are willing to pass on knowledge and information, because they have a genuine desire to share their passion.

When I was a small child, my mother would tell me that I asked too many questions, and I really haven't changed. I am endlessly inquisitive, especially when it comes to food, and have a burning desire to learn everything I can about produce and cooking. Plus, I seem to have an amazing capacity to forget and need to relearn my craft, which never ceases to amaze me!

As a cook, it is important for me to move forward, to always maintain an inquisitiveness, to try new things. When employing new young cooks in the kitchen, I don't look for speed, knife skills, or even organizational ability, although the latter is important on some level. Instead, I am more interested in how they react to the produce as it arrives. Do they look excited and inspired? Do they handle ingredients gently, with respect and appreciation? If the answers are yes, then I know we will work well together.

Since writing my first book, *A Year in My Kitchen*, my cooking has evolved in subtle ways that would probably pass unnoticed to anyone else. It has become simpler, more produce inspired. Flavors are now more inclined to whisper rather than roar. Dishes are very definitely layered still, but those layers are lighter, cleaner, and perhaps more ethereal. As I have grown in confidence, I find myself paring down my cooking, interfering less if you like. My intention is to make the produce taste even more of itself and the season to which it belongs.

More than ever I welcome in the new season's produce, which arrives almost on a weekly basis through the year. It makes me excited and smile when the first peach of the year perfectly ripens in one of our greenhouses, or winter purslane makes an appearance after nine months of absence. Tomatoes are greeted with great cheer in midsummer, yet come late fall I'm ready to pick black leaf kale after the first frost of the year. There is no better way of understanding what each season has to offer than to have a vegetable garden, however small.

My Favorite Ingredients highlights some of the rich and beautiful ingredients that I am privileged to work with throughout the culinary year. Most of the recipes are simple in their execution. For certain, there are no daunting or complicated techniques—just simple ways of combining good produce in order to maximize and fully appreciate its flavors. In keeping with my reverence for the seasons, starring ingredients are married with ingredients that are around at the same time, for nature cleverly provides perfectly balanced partners.

Many of the dishes are part of our repertoire at the restaurant. Beans and grains, nuts, game birds, fish and shellfish, and seasonal fruits and vegetables feature strongly in our dishes, along with abundant fresh herbs and beautiful olive oils. This type of cooking requires a warm-hearted approach and attention to the senses, but most importantly of all, it calls for an awe-inspiring reverence of the bounty this earth creates. Enjoy...

Cooking is not about being the best or most perfect cook, but rather it is about sharing the table with family and friends.

Asparagus

I am always eager for the first box of English asparagus to arrive. The season traditionally straddles May and early June, and lasts just six weeks in total, but it can vary a little. Young asparagus spears are the tender shoots of a much larger plant, which if left alone will grow more than three feet tall, with fernlike fronds and brilliant vermillion-colored berries. As the spears start poking their fine heads above the ground in early spring, they are generally harvested when bright green and no more than eight to ten inches high.

White asparagus is, in fact, the same plant, whose shoots have been banked by earth as they grow, keeping the spears underground and preventing them from turning green. In this way, the asparagus is blanched and the spears grow plump, smooth, and white except for their tips, which are tinged violet.

Asparagus is generally graded by size and sold in bunches. Size varies from stalks that are no thicker than fine pencils to ones that are as large and fat as Havana cigars.

Like most vegetables, asparagus starts to lose its sweetness as soon as it is picked from the ground, so it is important to choose the freshest possible specimens. Spears should be firm, smooth, and brightly colored with a vibrant bloom to the stem. Look for heads that are tightly formed and compact. All too often asparagus is picked after it has bolted. If this is the case, the buds will have begun to open and spread apart and the tiny branches under the heads will have opened up. Avoid asparagus like this, as it will usually be tougher and possibly taste a little bitter. Also check that the cut ends are not dry and white, indicating that they have not been freshly cut.

Now I associate asparagus with gentle warmth and dappled skies, but one of my abiding childhood memories is of eating canned asparagus on sweltering Christmas days in Australia. It was always cold from the refrigerator and so soggy that it would disintegrate in the mouth, yet strangely I enjoyed the flavor at the time.

Use asparagus as soon as possible after buying. If you need to store it briefly, treat it like cut flowers—stand the spears upright in a jar of water and place in the refrigerator.

◊

To prepare asparagus for cooking, grasp each spear between both hands and snap it. It will break at the woody end—just above where the stalk will be tender. You can save the woody ends for flavoring soup. I like to peel the lower part of the stalks if they are anything other than very slender. The skin on larger asparagus, in particular, tends to be tougher and slightly fibrous. Asparagus is easy to peel using a swivel vegetable peeler; it takes seconds and is well worth the effort.

◊

To boil asparagus, simply plunge into well-salted boiling water and cook until just tender when pierced with a knife. Cooking time will depend largely on the size and thickness of the spears, but as a general rule of thumb, it should take about 1½ minutes, and no longer than 3 minutes. When cooked, asparagus should take on an intense green color. White asparagus, which is much thicker, can take up to 8 minutes to cook through. Once cooked, serve at once or cool quickly, by draining and spreading the spears out on a board, so that they retain their lovely, appealing color. Asparagus is also delicious simply brushed with oil, seasoned, and cooked over a grill or broiler; it takes no longer than a few minutes.

We don't grow asparagus in our vegetable garden, mainly because it takes up a lot of space to produce a small harvest—almost 3 feet per plant. Also, grown from seed it takes 4 to 5 years to produce the first spears—a real test of patience. Nevertheless, we buy English green and French white asparagus in season, using both varieties in as many ways as we can, firstly because they are delicious, and secondly because they signal the arrival of spring.

Asparagus with Tabasco butter

I make a lot of flavored butters—they are a really good way to enhance simply broiled meat, fish, and vegetables. The possible flavorings are endless, from the famous café de Paris butter that has just about everything in it, to this very simple butter. We most often serve it with cracked crab claws, but in spring we sometimes use it for this simple appetizer.

Serves 4

about 32 green asparagus spears

freshly ground black pepper

Tabasco butter

scant 1 cup unsalted butter, at room temperature

1 heaping tbsp Dijon mustard

25 drops of Tabasco

juice of 1/2 lemon

sea salt

First make the flavored butter. Place the butter in a blender along with the mustard, Tabasco, lemon juice, and a good pinch of salt. Whiz until all the ingredients are well combined. Remove from the blender and spoon the butter into a small bowl. Cover and place in the refrigerator. Return to room temperature when ready to use. (This butter can be made a day or so in advance.)

To cook the asparagus, bring a large pot of well-salted water to a boil. Snap the woody ends off the asparagus, and peel the bottom 2 inches or so of the stalks, using a swivel vegetable peeler. When the water is boiling vigorously, drop in the asparagus and cook for 1 1/2 minutes, or until it is just tender to the bite. Remove with tongs and place in a warm bowl.

Add half the flavored butter and toss with the asparagus, then season with a little pepper.

Divide among warm plates and dot each pile of asparagus with a piece of the remaining butter. Serve while still piping hot.

Perfectly cooked green asparagus has a majestic flavor and texture, but if overcooked, it can be very disappointing. Don't leave the pan unattended during cooking—asparagus takes very little time to become tender, while retaining a bite, which is what you are aiming for.

Asparagus with tomato dressing and crème fraîche

This is a lovely asparagus appetizer. The tomato dressing has an intensity that contrasts well with the slightly nutty flavor of briefly cooked asparagus—and soft, gentle crème fraîche bridges the gap between the two flavors beautifully.

Serves 4

about 32 green or white asparagus spears

sea salt and freshly ground black pepper

1 tbsp extra virgin olive oil

4 tbsp crème fraîche

Tomato dressing

12 little ripe tomatoes

generous 3/4 cup extra virgin olive oil, plus extra to drizzle

sea salt and freshly ground black pepper

2 rosemary sprigs, leaves only

1 clove garlic, peeled

4 good-quality canned anchovy fillets in olive oil, drained

1 tbsp Dijon mustard

1 tbsp good-quality red wine vinegar

To finish

rosemary sprigs with flowers or minced parsley

First make the tomato dressing. Preheat the oven to 425°F (convection oven to 400°F). Pierce each tomato once with a small sharp knife—this helps to release the juice while the tomatoes are cooking. Place them in a roasting pan in which they fit quite snugly. Drizzle over a little olive oil and season with salt and pepper. Roast on the middle shelf of the oven until the tomatoes are soft and bursting from their skins, 15 to 20 minutes. Set aside to cool.

Pound the rosemary leaves, garlic, and anchovy fillets to a rough paste, using a mortar and pestle. Add the cooled tomatoes one by one, pounding after each addition, until all have been incorporated. Add the mustard and vinegar and stir well to combine. Pour in the 3/4 cup olive oil, stirring as you do so. Taste and season with a little salt and pepper. The dressing should be quite coarse and textural. Set aside to allow the flavors to adjust to each other.

To cook the asparagus, bring a large pot of well-salted water to a boil. Snap the woody ends off the asparagus, and peel the bottom 2 inches or so of the stalks, using a swivel vegetable peeler. When the water is boiling vigorously, drop in the asparagus and cook for 1¹/₂ minutes, or until it is just tender to the bite. Remove with tongs and place in a warm bowl.

Immediately season the asparagus with salt and pepper and dress with the olive oil. Arrange on warm plates, add a dollop of crème fraîche, and spoon on the tomato dressing. Finish with rosemary flowers, if available, or sprinkle with a little minced parsley and serve.

Asparagus, rice, and pancetta soup

Rather more of a really wet sloppy risotto than a soup, this is one of my all-time favorite recipes. It is rich and robust, with its roots definitely earthbound. Very, very satisfying.

Serves 4

1/4 cup extra virgin olive oil, plus extra to serve

2 red onions, peeled and minced

small bunch of thyme, leaves only

sea salt and freshly ground black pepper

5 slices of pancetta, chopped into small pieces

3 cloves garlic, peeled and crushed

1/2 cup white rice

4 cups chicken stock

2 cups water

12 green asparagus spears

4 ounces Parmesan, grated

2 tbsp chopped parsley

Warm the olive oil in a heavy pan large enough to hold all of the ingredients comfortably. Add the onions, thyme, and a pinch of salt and sweat over gentle heat for 10 minutes until the onions are soft, sweet, and translucent.

Add the pancetta pieces with the garlic and cook for another 5 to 10 minutes, then add the rice and stir well. Immediately pour in the stock and water, and bring to a simmer. Turn down the heat to fairly low, cover the pan, and cook until the rice is firm but evenly cooked; this will take about 20 minutes.

While the rice is cooking, prepare the asparagus. Snap the woody ends off the asparagus, and peel the bottom 2 inches or so of the stalks, using a swivel vegetable peeler. Then slice the stalks on the diagonal into short lengths. Add the asparagus to the soup and cook for 2 to 3 minutes until it is just tender. Add the Parmesan and stir. Season to taste with plenty of black pepper and a good pinch of salt.

Ladle the soup into warm soup plates, sprinkle with the parsley, and drizzle with a generous spoonful of olive oil.

In the kitchen I talk a lot about using the right size pots and pans. An overcrowded pan really doesn't make for good food in my opinion. I like heavy pans that are wide at the bottom with sides that are relatively low. I find it hard to make a connection with the food I am cooking if I have to peer too deeply into a pan!

Asparagus with ginger and garlic

Served simply with some plain steamed white rice, this is perfect for a light lunch or supper. In the springtime I often make this dish when I get home from work, tired but not necessarily very hungry. I find it a light, clean, stimulating supper. It is also very good as an accompaniment to white fish.

Serves 4

12 to 16 green asparagus spears

3/4- to 11/4-inch piece of fresh ginger

1 tbsp sunflower oil

1 clove garlic, peeled and finely sliced

1 fresh red chile, seeded and finely sliced

scant 1/3 cup water

11/2 tbsp oyster sauce, or to taste

freshly ground black pepper

Snap the woody ends off the asparagus and peel the bottom 2 inches or so of the stalks, using a swivel vegetable peeler. Then cut the spears on the diagonal into 11/2-inch lengths. Peel the ginger and slice into fine circles, then into the finest possible sticks.

Place a wok over medium-low heat and add the sunflower oil. When it is warm, add the ginger and cook for a few moments to release the flavor.

Add the asparagus, garlic, and chile, and toss to mix, then pour in the water and turn the heat to high. Cook for a minute, then add the oyster sauce. Toss well to coat the asparagus and cook for another 30 seconds or so until it is tender but retains a bite.

Remove from the heat and taste for seasoning. It shouldn't need any salt as the oyster sauce will give it all the saltiness it needs, but you might like to add a grinding of pepper. Serve very hot.

Asparagus with agretti, chili oil, and poached skate

Agretti is a tangy marsh grass, which—like asparagus—is in season during the spring and the two are natural partners. If you can't find agretti, then use young spinach instead, blanching it for a few seconds only until barely wilted. Delicate poached skate is wonderful served at room temperature with these vibrant vegetables. A drizzle of chili oil adds a touch of warmth to the finished dish.

Serves 4

14 ounces skate wings

mild-tasting extra virgin olive oil, to drizzle

sea salt and freshly ground black pepper

lemon juice, to taste

12 green or white asparagus spears

bunch of agretti

Poaching liquor

2 carrots, peeled and chopped

1 leek, green and white parts, trimmed, washed, and chopped

2 celery stalks, chopped

2 bay leaves

4 parsley sprigs

few thyme sprigs

5 black peppercorns

Chili oil

1 red bell pepper

4 fresh red chiles

sea salt

juice of 1/2 lemon

1 1/4 cups mild-tasting extra virgin olive oil

To serve

lemon wedges

For the poaching liquor, put a pan of water on to boil (one that is large enough to hold all the ingredients). Add the carrots, leek, and celery, along with the herbs and peppercorns. Once the water has returned to a boil, carefully add the skate wings and immediately turn off the heat. Allow the fish to cook in the residual heat of the poaching liquor as it cools.

When the fish is warm (no longer too hot to handle), carefully remove it using a slotted spoon and place in a bowl. Using your fingers, slide the flesh from its fanlike cartilage framework and break into shreds with your fingers. Place in a bowl and dress with a little olive oil. Season lightly with salt and pepper and finish with a few drops of lemon juice. Set aside while you make the chili oil.

Preheat the broiler to high and broil the bell pepper until the skin is charred and blistered all over, turning as necessary. Place it in a bowl, cover tightly with plastic wrap, and set aside; the steam will help to lift the skin. Do the same with the chiles, which will blacken much more quickly. When cool, peel off the skin from the bell pepper and chiles—it should come away easily. Slice in half and scrape out the core and seeds.

Pound the bell pepper and chiles with a good pinch of salt to a rough paste, using a mortar and pestle. Add the lemon juice and pour in the olive oil, stirring well to combine. You should have a vibrant, orangey-red, thick sludgy sauce. Set aside while you cook the asparagus and agretti.

Snap the woody ends off the asparagus and peel the bottom 2 inches or so of the stalks, using a swivel vegetable peeler. Put a large pot of well-salted water on to boil. Wash the agretti in several changes of cold water and pick over, chopping off the pink woody ends and removing any less-than-perfect fronds. When the water is boiling, plunge in the agretti and cook for a minute, then remove with a slotted spoon to a bowl. Dress, while still warm, with a little olive oil. Now cook the asparagus in the same water for 2 minutes. Drain and dress also with a little oil.

To assemble, put the agretti and asparagus into a bowl, add the
poached skate, and toss very gently to combine. Season with a little
salt and pepper and add a few drops of lemon juice. Arrange on
individual plates and lightly spoon over the chili oil. Serve with
lemon wedges for squeezing.

Gratin of white asparagus

This rich, creamy gratin of beautiful white asparagus wrapped in a cozy blanket is delicious paired with a simple roast chicken. A leafy green salad—tossed with a dressing that has a note of acidity—is the only other accompaniment you need. Alternatively, you can serve this gratin as it is, with some warm bread to mop up the sauce and, perhaps, some finely sliced porcini mushrooms on the side, dressed with no more than beautiful olive oil, sea salt, and black pepper.

Serves 4

4 1/2 tbsp unsalted butter, melted

15 white asparagus spears

small bunch of lemon thyme, leaves only

generous 3/4 cup crème fraîche

1 tbsp Dijon mustard

sea salt and freshly ground black pepper

1 cup fresh white bread crumbs

3 1/2 ounces Parmesan, freshly grated

2 tbsp minced curly parsley

Preheat the oven to 450°F (convection oven to 425°F). Brush a copper or ceramic gratin dish with a little of the melted butter.

Trim the asparagus: you will find that white asparagus needs to be trimmed much higher—roughly halfway up the stalks, as a rule of thumb. Slice the spears in half lengthwise and lay them in the buttered gratin dish. Sprinkle with most of the lemon thyme leaves, saving a few for garnish.

Now put the crème fraîche and mustard into a heavy pan and place over medium heat. Stir to combine and bring to a simmer, then turn down the heat slightly and let bubble to reduce by about a quarter. Season the reduced mixture with salt and pepper to taste.

Meanwhile, put the bread crumbs in a bowl, add the Parmesan, parsley, and some pepper, and toss with your fingers to combine.

Pour the mustardy crème fraîche over the asparagus, then scatter the crumb mixture on top, distributing it evenly. Drizzle over the rest of the melted butter. Bake the gratin on the middle shelf of the oven until the top is crisp and golden and the cream bubbles up around the sides of the dish, 15 to 20 minutes. Sprinkle with the remaining thyme leaves and serve.

It is important not to overcook this dish—the asparagus should retain a bite and nuttiness. Overcooking could make the spears seem as though they have come out of a can.

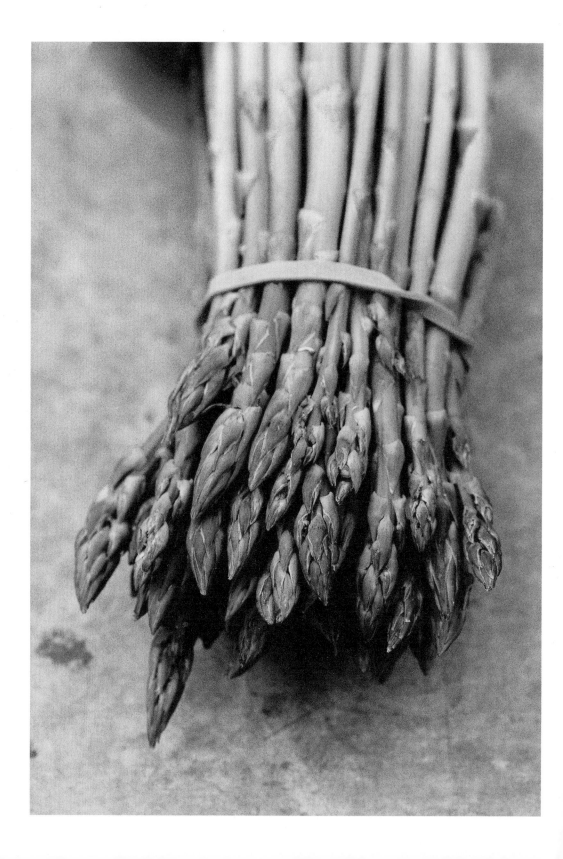

Grilled lamb steak with asparagus and a salsa verde of lovage

The vast and wild lovage plant that looms over one corner of our vegetable garden seems to grow taller every day, no matter how much we cut it down to use in the kitchen. To me, lovage has a strong and very English taste—like peppery celery. It is good used sparingly in soups and salads, or as here, coarsely chopped in a green sauce to be spooned over grilled lamb. Be aware though that its flavor can easily be overpowering. This is a nice dish to eat outdoors on a warm spring day.

Serves 4

4 boneless lamb steaks, cut from the upper leg, each about 6 ounces and 3/4 inch thick, trimmed of most fat

sea salt and freshly ground black pepper

olive oil, to rub

20 green or white asparagus spears

1 tbsp extra virgin olive oil

Salsa verde

1 tbsp good-quality capers packed in salt, well rinsed

1 clove garlic, peeled and crushed

1 tbsp Dijon mustard

1 1/2 tbsp red wine vinegar

12 lovage leaves

bunch of Italian parsley

handful of arugula leaves

sea salt and freshly ground black pepper

generous 3/4 cup extra virgin olive oil

Lay the lamb steaks on a board and season well all over with 1 1/2 tbsp salt. It sounds like a lot of salt, but do use it all. Cover the lamb and let stand in the refrigerator for at least 24 hours, but up to 3 days is good. This will tenderize the meat and give it a wonderful seasoned flavor right to its very core.

Remove the meat from the refrigerator an hour before cooking, to allow it to return to room temperature. Brush off any excess salt.

Meanwhile, make the sauce, preferably by hand. Roughly chop the capers and place them in a bowl with the garlic, mustard, and vinegar. Wash the lovage, parsley, and arugula, pat dry, and chop fairly finely, ensuring that there is still plenty of texture. Add to the bowl with a pinch of salt and some pepper. Pour over the olive oil and stir well to combine. Set aside.

When ready to cook, heat up your grill or broiler. When it is really hot, rub the meat all over with olive oil. Grill or broil for just 4 minutes on one side without turning, then turn and cook for another 4 minutes on the other side. The meat should have a lovely dark crust. Set aside to rest in a warm place for 10 minutes.

Meanwhile, cook the asparagus. Bring a large pot of well-salted water to a boil. Snap the woody ends off the asparagus, and peel the bottom 2 inches or so of the stalks, using a swivel vegetable peeler. When the water is boiling vigorously, drop in the asparagus and cook for 1 1/2 minutes, or until it is just tender to the bite. Drain and dress with the extra virgin olive oil and season with salt and pepper.

Slice each lamb steak into 3 slices on the diagonal. Divide the asparagus among warm serving plates, lay the lamb on top, and spoon over the salsa verde. Serve while still warm.

Cherries

The arrival of the first cherries marks the beginning of summer for me. In season from around June, cherries—along with apricots—are the first of the year's pit fruits to ripen. Yet strangely enough, cherries always remind me of Christmas, salt water, and mangoes. My memories of Christmas growing up in Australia are of heat, long summer vacations by the sea, and boxes brimming with cherries and mangoes that my mother would bring home from the local greengrocers. My sister, brother, and I would work through the first box of cherries in one sitting, our mother having shooed us outside so as not to make a mess. We'd gorge on handfuls of fruit, spitting the pits as far as we possibly could. I always hoped that one of those far-flung pits would miraculously grow into a tree that would produce endless fruit just for us ... but of course that never happened. I loved the taste of the sweet fragrant fruit, and my first ever pair of earrings was a pair of cherries hooked over the top of my ears!

There are more than 500 varieties of cherries in cultivation—their colors ranging from deep, dark red through pale yellow hues tinged with orange, to almost white. They can be broadly classified into sweet and sour cherries. My favorites lie among the paler varieties, whose flavor—even when perfectly ripe—has a gentle tartness. The darker varieties are juicy and wonderfully fragrant at their peak, but they seem to pass this point quickly and their flavor is soon overblown.

◊

When you are buying cherries, look for fruit that is bright, plump, and glossy, with flesh that is tight and plump. At farmers' markets and greengrocers they are often sold loose, so take time to pick through and take only the perfect ones. Check the stems, too—these should be green and crisp, not brown and woody. That said, the best way of finding out whether you've come across a good crop is to taste one.

◊

At the restaurant, we use both sweet and sour cherries. Of the sour varieties, morello is a particular favorite. We pickle these small, tart, deep red cherries in a solution of sherry or wine vinegar, sugar, and cloves, and keep them tightly sealed in a dark corner. In the early fall, we serve them alongside cured meats or tossed in warm salads. Game, such as grouse or pheasant, and the early bitter winter leaves pair well with pickled cherries, as do the first of the fall nuts—young soft walnuts and hazelnuts.

◊

When perfectly ripe and deliciously juicy, sweet cherries need no embellishment. If you can resist eating them straight from the bag, give them a quick rinse and savor them just as they are. Their season is brief—perhaps the briefest of all the summer fruits—lasting not much longer than a month, so make the most of them. Beyond enjoying them in their natural state, we also make sweet cherries into sorbets and ice creams, simple cordials, and tarts. To round off a simple, satisfying meal, I really can't think of anything better than a plate of fresh ripe cherries and juicy apricots with soft, lemony goat cheeses, drizzled lightly with fragrant honey.

Pickled cherries

We tend to make these with sour morello cherries, which we grow against the south-facing wall of our vegetable garden. Inedible raw, they are perfect for preserving. Over time, they become quite wrinkly in the pickling liquor, which I rather like. If you cannot get hold of these little sour cherries, pickle one of the sweet varieties instead.

Makes 2 or 3 18-ounce jars

2¼ pounds ripe cherries
3½ cups superfine sugar
3⅓ cups red wine vinegar
6 bay leaves
12 cloves
15 black peppercorns

Discard any blemished or bruised fruit, but leave the stems on as they look really pretty. Rinse the cherries and pat dry.

Dissolve the sugar in the vinegar in a large pan over low heat, then add the bay leaves, cloves, and peppercorns. Bring to a boil, lower the heat, and simmer for 10 minutes. Remove from the heat and let the syrup cool completely.

Pack the cherries loosely into warm sterilized jars and pour over the cooled syrup. Leave in a cool, dark cupboard for a couple of weeks before eating to let the flavors mellow, then refrigerate. They will keep in the refrigerator for up to a year.

Little clusters of grapes can be pickled in the same way. Proceed as above, adding 4 or 5 juniper berries to the pickling liquor. These grapes are lovely served with soft cheeses (see page 220).

Warm pheasant salad with tardivo, pickled cherries, and toasted hazelnuts

This is a lovely fall salad. Warm pheasant is delicious served with the first bittersweet leaves of the year, new season's nut oil, pickled cherries, and finely sliced fennel or celery to give a clean, watery crunch. Tardivo is a form of Treviso radicchio, with a sharper flavor, and you can use Treviso radicchio in its place.

Serves 4

1 pheasant, about 2¹/2 pounds

sea salt and freshly ground black pepper

2 tbsp olive oil

1 tardivo or radicchio, or a small bunch each of arugula and dandelion

1 fennel bulb

1 pomegranate

1¹/2 tbsp aged balsamic vinegar

1¹/2 tbsp extra virgin olive oil

few drops of lemon juice

small handful of chervil leaves, minced

Dressing

1 tbsp pickling liquor (from the cherries)

1 tbsp Dijon mustard

2 tsp sherry vinegar

sea salt and freshly ground black pepper

¹/4 cup hazelnut oil

2 tbsp mild-tasting extra virgin olive oil

To serve

about 12 pickled cherries (page 29)

20 hazelnuts, lightly toasted and roughly chopped (optional)

Preheat the oven to 350°F (convection oven to 350°F). Cut off the tips of the pheasant wings, using a sharp knife. Season the bird generously all over with salt and pepper. Heat the olive oil in a large nonstick pan over low heat and pan-fry the pheasant, turning until golden brown all over.

Lay the bird on one side in a shallow roasting pan and roast in the oven for 8 to 10 minutes, then turn onto the other side and roast for another 8 to 10 minutes. Now turn the bird breast side down and roast until cooked, 8 to 10 minutes. To check, pull a leg away from the breast and look for any sign of rawness; also make sure that the juices run clear. Set aside to rest, breast side down, for 15 minutes.

Meanwhile, for the salad, separate the tardivo leaves, wash, and gently pat dry, then place in a bowl. Remove the outer fibrous layer from the fennel, halve the bulb lengthwise, then slice into very fine shards. Add to the leaves. Cut the pomegranate in half, then hold, cut side down, over a bowl and tap to release the seeds, picking out any bits of membrane that fall into the bowl. Scatter over the leaves.

For the dressing, whisk the pickling liquor, mustard, vinegar, and a pinch each of salt and pepper together in a bowl. Gradually whisk in the oils, then taste and adjust the seasoning if necessary. You should have a slightly sweet, nutty, earthy vinaigrette.

While still warm, remove the pheasant flesh from the bones and place in a bowl. Toss with the balsamic vinegar, extra virgin olive oil, lemon juice, a little salt and pepper, and the chervil.

Now add the warm pheasant to the salad leaves and drizzle over a little of the dressing. Toss together lightly, using your fingertips, and arrange on serving plates. Scatter over the pickled cherries and hazelnuts, drizzle with a little more vinaigrette, and serve at once.

Clafoutis

When cherries are in season and really ripe, make this lovely light, comforting dessert. Don't bother to remove the pits—they make for a better flavor and are easily removed on eating.

Serves 6

3 tbsp unsalted butter

1 1/3 pounds sweet cherries, washed and stems removed

1/2 cup superfine sugar, plus 3 tbsp

1/2 tsp ground cinnamon

grated zest of 1 lemon

2 organic eggs, separated

1/2 cup all-purpose flour

scant 1 cup ground almonds

1 tsp vanilla extract

generous 1/3 cup heavy cream

sea salt

Melt the butter in a small pan over medium heat. When it is foaming (but not browned), add the cherries, 1/2 cup of the sugar, the cinnamon, and lemon zest. Cook gently for 10 minutes or until the cherries are soft, stirring gently from time to time. The juices should have reduced and thickened slightly. Remove from the heat.

Using a slotted spoon, spoon two-thirds of the fruit over the bottom of a shallow 9-inch round baking pan; set aside the rest of the cherries in the juice for serving.

Preheat the oven to 425°F (convection oven to 400°F). Beat the egg yolks and the remaining 3 tbsp sugar together in a large bowl until light and fluffy. Beat in the flour, almonds, vanilla, and cream. In a separate clean bowl, whisk the egg whites with a pinch of salt until they form soft peaks.

Carefully fold the whisked egg whites into the batter until they are just evenly incorporated, then pour the mixture over the cherries. Bake on the top shelf of the oven until the batter is puffed and golden brown, 15 to 20 minutes.

Let the clafoutis cool slightly for 5 minutes or so before serving, topped with the reserved cherries and juice.

I add a little salt to many of the desserts that I make, because I find it keeps the sweetness in check and pulls back fruits to their real flavor, which sugar has a tendency to mask.

Vanilla ice cream with poached cherries and chocolate sauce

Cherries, chocolate, and vanilla ice cream seem to me to belong together, so I've combined them here to make a simple, light-hearted dessert. You could add some sliced banana and toasted chopped nuts for a sundae if you like. The ice cream can be made a day or two ahead, but preferably no longer.

Serves 6

Vanilla ice cream
scant 2 cups heavy cream
2/3 cup whole milk
1 vanilla bean, split lengthwise
6 organic egg yolks
2/3 cup superfine sugar

Poached cherries
1 pound 2 ounces cherries
1 cup superfine sugar
juice of 1 lemon
1 tbsp Pedro Ximénez sherry

Chocolate sauce
4 1/2 ounces good-quality dark, bitter chocolate (minimum 68% cocoa solids), grated
1/2 cup heavy cream
1/2 cup whole milk
1 tsp honey

To finish
handful of fresh cherries with stalks, washed

To make the ice cream, pour the cream and milk into a heavy pan and place over low heat. Scrape the seeds from the vanilla bean and add them to the creamy milk with the empty bean. Slowly bring to just below a boil, remove from the heat, and set aside to infuse for 15 minutes.

In the meantime, beat the egg yolks and sugar together in a large bowl with a whisk until pale. Gently reheat the creamy milk and pour onto the egg yolk mixture, stirring with the whisk as you do so. Return to the pan.

Stir the custard over the lowest possible heat until it thickens. This will take 8 to 10 minutes (don't be tempted to increase the heat, or the custard will curdle). As soon as it is thick enough to lightly coat the back of a wooden spoon, remove from the heat and pour into a bowl. Let cool, then churn in an ice-cream maker until thick. Unless using straightaway, transfer to a plastic container and store in the freezer.

For the poached cherries, rinse the fruit, remove the stems, and place in a pan with the sugar and lemon juice. Bring to a simmer, then cover and poach gently for 10 minutes, or until the cherries are very tender and have released a lot of liquid. Using a slotted spoon, transfer the cherries to a bowl. Add the sherry to the pan, turn up the heat, and boil vigorously for 2 minutes. Pour over the fruit and let cool slightly (while you make the sauce) or leave until cold.

For the chocolate sauce, combine all the ingredients in a pan and heat gently, stirring until smooth. Remove from the heat and let cool slightly.

To serve, layer the vanilla ice cream, poached cherries, and warm chocolate sauce alternately in pretty glasses. Top with a few fresh cherries and serve at once.

Cherry granita

This lovely, vibrant, fairy floss pink granita is the perfect end to a simple lunch on a warm day in June. The sweet icy granules tingle on your tongue, releasing a taste that is pure cherry. The fruit is uncooked in this recipe, allowing the cleanest possible flavor of cherry to shine through.

Serves 6 to 8

3 pounds ripe, sweet cherries
2 cups superfine sugar
generous 1 cup water
small pinch of sea salt
lemon juice

Wash the cherries and pat dry, then remove the stems and pits. Tip the fruit into a food processor and purée until smooth. Pass through a strainer into a bowl and set aside.

Place the sugar and water in a heavy pan over medium heat. Once the sugar has dissolved, turn up the heat slightly and simmer for 3 to 4 minutes, or until the syrup is slightly viscous. Remove from the heat and let cool completely.

When cold, pour the syrup over the puréed cherries. Add the salt, squeeze in a few drops of lemon juice, and stir well to combine. Pour into a shallow freezerproof tray—the purée should be no more than 1$\frac{1}{4}$ inches thick. Cover and freeze for an hour or so.

When the granita begins to set and has firmed up around the edges, remove from the freezer and use a fork to drag the frozen crystals from the edges in toward the center. Don't beat the mixture—a granita is meant to be icy and crunchy, not smooth like a sorbet.

Return to the freezer for another 30 minutes or so, then repeat the procedure. Now freeze until set. Store in a covered plastic container in the freezer until ready to use. To serve, scrape shavings from the granita and pile into chilled glasses.

Perfectly ripe fruit is generally better showcased in a granita rather than a sorbet, because the latter requires more sugar to set smoothly and the more sugar that is added, the more the true flavor of the fruit is masked.

Brandied cherries

These little translucent ruby jewels shine from their glass jars, giving a sense of comfort and warmth to everyone who sets eyes on them. Every year we lay a few fruits in brandy—usually cherries, damson plums, and raspberries—primarily so that we can enjoy their taste and beauty a little longer than their natural season allows. The brandy will eventually overwhelm the delicate flavor of the fruit, but they will last for up to a year in the refrigerator. Choose fruit in really good condition, without bruises, soft spots, or blemishes.

Makes 2¹/4 pounds

2¹/4 pounds ripe cherries
1³/4 cups brandy, such as an aged apple brandy
scant 3/4 cup superfine sugar
¹/2 cup water

Wash the cherries, leaving on their stems, and lay them out to dry on a clean cloth.

Pour the brandy into a small pan and add the sugar and water. Heat gently to dissolve the sugar and warm the liquor.

Pack the cherries loosely into one large sterilized jar or a couple of smaller ones. Pour the warmed brandy over the cherries, making sure that the fruit is totally submerged in the alcohol. Seal and store in a cool, dark place for a week or so to let the flavors develop, then store in the refrigerator.

We use brandied cherries in a variety of sweet and savory dishes: with quail, pigeon or pâté, bitter leaves, and fall nuts; warmed through and served with duck breast; with thinly sliced raw fennel, toasted hazelnuts, and a rich, creamy cheese, such as robiola; sautéed quickly in a pan with a little butter, a touch of sugar, and some syrup from the jar to tumble warm over vanilla ice cream; with broiled fresh apricots and a dollop of sweetened mascarpone; paired with chunks of dark chocolate and a biscotti or two, for an elegant, lazy dessert.

Cherry cordial

I love making cordials, as they are celebratory in feel and look beautiful served in pitchers on the table for everyone to share. You can adapt this simple recipe to almost any seasonal fruit, including quince, black currants, raspberries, and blackberries.

Makes about 4 cups

2¹/4 pounds ripe cherries

scant 13/4 cups
superfine sugar

grated zest of 1 lemon

4 cups water

1 tbsp rose syrup

To serve
still or sparkling water
crushed ice

Wash the cherries and pat dry, then remove the stems. Tip the fruit into a medium heavy pan and add the sugar, lemon zest, and water. Bring to a boil over medium heat, then turn down the heat and simmer gently for 15 minutes, or until the cherries are tender and have bled their color into the water. Remove from the heat and let cool slightly.

Strain through a fine strainer into a bowl, pressing down on the fruit with the back of a ladle to extract as much juice as possible. Let the strained syrup cool completely, then add the rose syrup and stir well to combine. Pour into a sterilized bottle or jar and store in the refrigerator for up to a week.

To serve, dilute the cordial with still or sparkling water, as you prefer, and serve with lots of crushed ice on a hot day.

Fish & shellfish

I love fish of all description. Their clean, clear flavors appeal to me and I've become increasingly confident in cooking them. The variety is endless, from spanking fresh oily fish—like sardines, mackerel, and anchovies—to the more subtle white-fleshed species—such as halibut, bass, and sole. The largest of the white flatfish, turbot— affectionately known as the king of the sea—can be considered somewhat in between in the kitchen. It has rich, succulent white flesh that can take the intense flavors of porcini, chanterelles, or even bone marrow.

I am particularly fond of shellfish, especially juicy king scallops, sweet crab, and luscious lobsters. And I love the way mussels and clams add their distinctive flavor to everything they come in contact with. Bread is an essential partner to these bivalves—to mop up every trace of their delicious briny juices.

Just as all things worth eating have a time and place in which they are at their very best, so does fish. Lobster, for example, is beautiful in the spring and fall when its flesh is firm and sweet. Mussels are at their prime in the fall. Their beautiful appearance and plump, orange flesh—tasting of the sea—make me eager to devour them. They work well with strong, clear flavors, such as ripe tomatoes, chile, garlic, rosemary, and wine vinegar. Surprisingly though, mussels are equally good with the delicate flavors of saffron, white wine, and crème fraîche. Clams, too, though they can seem fussy to eat, lend a superb flavor to the most basic of dishes. Linguine with vongole (clams), for example, is merely pasta tossed with clams, garlic, a little dried chile, a splash of white wine, and lashings of good grassy olive oil... yet it is a dish fit for a king.

There is much to say on the virtues of our other shellfish—noble lobster and delicate crab, of course, but also beautiful scallops, with their plump sweet flesh. I love to eat them with garlicky butter or tossed with an array of winter leaves. Saltwater Poole shrimp that arrive in September are another favorite. These are so tiny and full of flavor, they need nothing more than a squeeze of lemon juice, a sprinkling of salt, and perhaps a few slivers of fresh red chile.

◊

As for oily fish—anchovies, sardines, mackerel, and herring—these are delicious without question, as long as they are very fresh. Their lovely, oily flesh spoils quickly, so they need to be eaten soon after you buy them—preferably the same day, or at least within 24 hours. They also need to be served piping hot. Vinegar cuts through their strong flavors successfully, as does horseradish, and a sweet foil of tomatoes or beets and a sprinkling of salt is vital for these fish.

◊

Wild halibut, caught off the coast of Scotland, is quite simply the cleanest and whitest of all fish, with a beautiful texture. It marries well with just about anything—from tandoor spices to a simple accompaniment of spinach dressed with olive oil and a good squeeze of lemon. Wild salmon, in season from mid-spring through early summer, is only ever a rare treat. Its deep orangey pink flesh has a delicate richness, which I adore. Baked whole in salt, it is a delight served with freshly made mayonnaise and young peppery arugula, or the first new potatoes of the year pulled straight from the ground—and perhaps a plate of sliced ripe tomatoes.

Turbot—rich and gelatinous—is a different beast altogether. It benefits from being cooked on the bone and can carry stronger flavors. One way to cook it is with porcini mushrooms, sourdough bread crumbs, and bone marrow—a lovely elegant dish to serve in the colder months. And then there is wild bass and sea bream, and beautiful red mullet with its distinctive flavor of the sea... so many tempting options.

Lastly I must not forget monkfish, the great pretender, known as poor man's lobster in France because its flesh is more reminiscent of a crustacean than a white fish. Firm, meaty, and bouncy, with only one central bone to remove, it is delicious served with white beans laced with tomatoes and tarragon or in a rustic fish stew.

◊

The wealth of the sea is truly breathtaking and seemingly endless, which brings me to one final, very important consideration. Of this rich bounty we must take care, for its ecosystem has become so very fragile. The waters of the world have been ruthlessly overfished and supplies are dwindling on a frightening scale. We must take from them wisely and carefully—sustainably. I urge you to seek out fish that have been line caught, close to our shores. Ask your fishmonger where his fish has come from—has it been caught by local day boats rather than deep-sea trawlers? Steer clear of species during their spawning season, and at other times avoid taking too much of any one of them. Be aware of endangered species—wild salmon, halibut, monkfish, etc.—and eat them rarely. It is vital, so that we—and those who come after us—may be able to continue to enjoy them.

We use diver scallops at the restaurant, each one individually picked by someone, as opposed to trawled in nets that are dragged along the bottom of the sea, damaging just about everything they come into contact with.

Shrimp with chile, salt, and lemon

We deep-fry delicious little shrimp in the hottest oil until crunchy and eat them whole—piping hot and sprinkled generously with salt. I encourage you to do the same—please don't bother to peel them as the flavor is all in the shell.

20 to 30 little shrimp per person (depending on size)

corn oil, to deep-fry

sea salt

1 fresh red chile, seeded and finely sliced (optional)

lemon juice

Rinse the shrimp and pat thoroughly dry with paper towels. Heat the corn oil in a deep-fat fryer or other suitable heavy pan to 340°F; check the temperature with an instant-read thermometer.

Cook the shrimp in several batches: Add to the hot oil and cook for 1 to 2 minutes, or until bright red in color and crunchy in texture. Remove with a slotted spoon and drain on paper towels while you deep-fry the rest. Season generously with sea salt and sprinkle over the sliced chile if using. Finish with a good squeeze of lemon juice.

These crunchy shrimp are delicious as a predinner nibble with a glass of Champagne.

My choice of oil for deep-frying is corn oil, because it cooks evenly and has a neutral taste that doesn't interfere with the taste of the food I am cooking.

Crab cakes with corn purée and chili oil

These little, light crab cakes are unusual in that they are simply fresh crabmeat flavored with a few aromatics and bound with rich, unctuous homemade mayonnaise. They sing of summer, especially when served with a purée of sweet, fresh corn—the perfect foil for richly flavored crab. Add a squeeze of lime and a drizzle of chili oil to make this dish just about perfect!

Makes 8 little cakes

9 ounces fresh crabmeat

1 fresh red chile, seeded and diced

1 tbsp minced cilantro leaves

1/3 cup mayonnaise (page 182; use the juice of 1 lemon and omit the balsamic vinegar)

lime or lemon juice

sea salt

1 cup fresh white bread crumbs

1/2 cup plus 2 tbsp unsalted butter

Chili oil

1 fresh red chile, seeded and finely diced

sea salt

scant 1/3 cup extra virgin olive oil

Corn purée

3 fresh corn cobs, outer husks removed

1/2 cup water

3 tbsp unsalted butter

2 tsp sugar

sea salt and freshly ground black pepper

1/4 cup crème fraîche

1 tsp Tabasco, or to taste

To serve

lime wedges

Put the crabmeat into a bowl, add the chile and cilantro, and fork through to distribute evenly. Add the mayonnaise and stir well to combine—it not only enriches the flavor of the crab, but also binds it together. Add a squeeze of lime or lemon juice and enough salt to bring out all the flavors. Form the mixture into 8 little cakes and place on a baking sheet. Chill for 30 minutes to firm up slightly.

Spread the bread crumbs evenly on a board and roll the crab cakes in them to coat generously. Cover and refrigerate until needed.

For the chili oil, put the diced chile into a bowl, add a good pinch of salt, and pour on the olive oil. Stir to combine and let infuse.

For the corn purée, cut the kernels from the cobs. The easiest way to do this is to stand the cob upright on a board and run a sharp knife down in sections. Discard any stringy bits. Tip the corn kernels into a pan; add the water, butter, and sugar; and season generously with salt and pepper. Cover and cook gently over medium heat until the corn is tender, 20 to 25 minutes, then drain, reserving the liquor.

Transfer half of the corn to a bowl, using a slotted spoon. Tip the rest into a blender or food processor and blend until smooth. Pass through a strainer into a bowl to ensure a really smooth purée; if it is too thick, stir in a little of the reserved liquor. Add to the rest of the corn and stir well. Add the crème fraîche and Tabasco and stir again. Check the seasoning and keep warm.

To cook the crab cakes, heat the butter in a wide nonstick pan over medium-low heat. When it is warm, gently lay the crab cakes in the pan and cook for about 2 minutes on each side until golden and crispy. Remove with a slotted spoon and drain on paper towels.

Serve the crab cakes piping hot, with the corn purée. Pass around the chili oil and lime wedges for squeezing.

Lobster salad with fennel and blood oranges

The clean crunch of fennel and winter leaves, such as Castelfranco or frisée, complements the sweet, rich flesh of lobster in this winter salad, and the sweet, citrus taste of blood oranges rounds off the dish perfectly. Crab also works well here, so you could substitute it for the lobster. These quantities are sufficient for an appetizer; to serve as a lunch or main course, allow one lobster each.

Serves 4

2 very fresh live lobsters, each about 1 pound 2 ounces

1/2 lemon

1/4 cup mild-tasting extra virgin olive oil (such as Sicilian or Ligurian)

sea salt and freshly ground black pepper

3 blood oranges

1/2 head Castelfranco or frisée

1 fennel bulb

bunch of young, tender agretti or arugula

small bunch of chervil, stems removed

aged balsamic vinegar, to drizzle

Keep the lobsters covered with a damp cloth in the refrigerator and cook soon after buying. An hour or so before cooking, place them in the freezer—the intense cold will send them into a deep sleep.

When ready to cook the lobsters, put a large pot of well-salted water on to boil—it should be almost as salty as the sea. When it comes to a rolling boil, drop in the lobsters and cook for 8 minutes exactly. The timing is important, as lobster meat is not at all good if it is overcooked. Remove the lobsters from the pan with tongs and set aside until they are cool enough to handle.

To remove the meat from the shell, first twist off the claws and tap the thickest part of these with a rolling pin to crack them open. Gently remove the claw shell, leaving the flesh intact if possible and set aside for serving. Now lay the body on its back on a board and, using a very sharp, large knife, cut through the middle of the soft underbelly to slice the tail meat in half lengthwise. You should then be able to remove the outer shell (rather like removing a coat). Season the flesh with a squeeze of lemon juice, a drizzle of olive oil, and a little salt and pepper.

Using a paring knife, cut away the skin and white pith from the oranges, then slice crosswise into pinwheels 1/8 inch thick, discarding the seeds. Separate the Castelfranco leaves, leaving small ones whole and roughly tearing larger ones, then wash and gently pat dry. Remove the tough outer layer of the fennel bulb, then halve lengthwise. Now slice each half lengthwise into fine slices and squeeze over a few drops of lemon juice to stop them discoloring.

To assemble the salad, place the fennel, Castelfranco, agretti, and chervil in a bowl with the lobster meat and toss lightly. Dress with the remaining lemon juice and olive oil. Taste and season with salt and pepper if needed.

Divide the salad among serving plates and arrange the blood orange slices on top. Finish with the reserved lobster claw flesh and drizzle with a little aged balsamic to serve.

Carpaccio of smoked haddock with chile and winter purslane

Finely sliced, very fresh fish served raw with a few carefully chosen flavorings makes a beautifully simple, elegant first course. The tastes here are clean and as light as air—so subtle that they linger for barely a moment before they evaporate. The seasoning needs to be quite generous—it is delicious to come across a crystally crunch of salt.

Serves 4

14 ounces smoked haddock fillet

juice of 1 lemon

1/4 cup very good–quality olive oil

1 fresh red chile, finely sliced

coarse sea salt

handful of purslane (or pea shoots or cress)

Lay the smoked haddock skin side down on a board. Using a very sharp knife, slice downward at an angle through the skin to cut into wafer-thin slices. As you cut, lay the haddock slices on a plate—overlapping them as you do so.

Sprinkle with the lemon juice, drizzle with the olive oil, and scatter over the chile. Season with salt to taste.

Finish with the purslane—not too much, as it should be little more than a palate-cleansing crunch. Serve immediately, before the lemon juice has a chance to "cook" the fish.

The gentle flavor of sweet smoky haddock is better experienced in its raw state in my view. I find the delicate texture of the raw flesh matches the ethereal flavor of the fish more appropriately.

Roasted halibut with preserved lemon and crème fraîche sauce

This combination of simply roasted firm-fleshed, white fish and preserved lemon is unfussy—both in its execution and taste, but it is very, very good! In late summer I love to eat it with sliced perfectly ripe tomatoes, drizzled with very good olive oil. In the cooler months, I like it with spinach—just wilted and flavored with a little finely sliced chile and a drizzle of olive oil.

Serves 4

1 tbsp olive oil

4 halibut fillets, about 6½ ounces each, with skin

sea salt and freshly ground black pepper

Sauce

2 preserved lemons

small bunch of mint, leaves only

small bunch of basil, leaves only

3 tbsp water

squeeze of lemon juice (if needed)

generous 3/4 cup crème fraîche

To serve

lemon wedges

First make the sauce. Cut the preserved lemons into quarters and rinse under cold running water, removing and discarding the flesh, which can taste bitter. You will be left with just the peel. Place this in a blender along with the herbs and water, and purée to a smooth paste. Transfer to a bowl and try a little—it should taste fragrant and distinctive, a little salty but not excessively so. If it seems a bit too salty, add a squeeze or two of lemon juice, otherwise don't bother. Stir in the crème fraîche and set aside in the refrigerator while you cook the fish.

Preheat the oven to 375°F (convection to 350°F). Place a large nonstick ovenproof pan over medium heat and add the olive oil. Season the fish generously with salt and pepper, seasoning the skin more than the flesh side. Once the pan is hot, lay the fish in it, skin side down. Cook, without touching or turning, for about 2 minutes until the skin is golden and has popped itself up from the bottom of the pan. Now place the pan in the oven (still without turning the fish) and cook for 2 to 4 minutes until just cooked through.

Remove from the oven (remembering to protect your hand with an oven mitt as the pan handle will be very hot). Lift the fish onto serving plates, placing the fillets skin side up. Spoon the cool lemony sauce on top and serve straightaway, with lemon wedges and whatever else you choose!

Never overcrowd a pan, especially when cooking fish. Food needs space and air around it to cook properly. If you think your pan might not be big enough, then use two pans or cook in batches. An overcrowded pan will only lead to food that is stewed, and its final taste will reflect that.

Salt-baked wild salmon with roasted tomato aïoli, potatoes, and purslane

This is a really good way to cook fish that is to be served whole for a large gathering. It allows a rich gelatinous, slightly oily fish to benefit from all the wonderful flavors that come from the bones. The salt coating sets firm, like clay, when it is mixed with water and exposed to high heat, so the fish steams beautifully inside its protective case. Ask your fishmonger to clean the fish but leave the scales on—they will prevent the salt from penetrating the fish as it cooks.

Serves 8 to 12

1 wild salmon, about
9 pounds, cleaned but
not scaled

2 lemons, thinly sliced

1 branch of wild fennel

11 pounds coarse rock salt

Tomato aïoli

3 organic egg yolks

2 cloves garlic, peeled and
crushed

juice of 1/2 lemon

sea salt and freshly ground
black pepper

6 to 8 slow-roasted tomatoes
(see page 123), cooled

scant 1/3 cup extra virgin
olive oil

Potatoes

2 1/4 pounds new potatoes,
washed

juice of 1/2 lemon

sea salt and freshly ground
black pepper

1/4 cup extra virgin olive oil

handful of purslane or
pea shoots

Start by making the aïoli. Place the egg yolks in a blender or food processor, add the garlic, lemon juice, a little salt and pepper, and the tomatoes, then whiz briefly to combine. With the motor running, pour in the olive oil in a slow, steady stream through the feeder tube. Taste and adjust the seasoning if necessary. (This can be made up to a day in advance.)

When you are ready to cook the salmon, preheat the oven to its highest setting, at least 500°F (convection oven to 475°F). Rinse the fish inside and out under cold running water, then pat it dry. Place the lemon slices inside the cavity, along with the fennel, but don't bother to season the fish.

Put the rock salt in a mixing bowl and add enough cold water to give the consistency of wet sand (as much as 4 cups, depending on the type of salt). Mix together with your hands.

Spread half of the salt mix on a large baking sheet or in a shallow roasting pan to create a flat, even surface. Lay the fish on top and cover with the rest of the salt, packing it firmly around the fish (as if you were burying someone at the beach!).

Place on the middle shelf of the hot oven and bake for 15 to 20 minutes, or until the fish is barely cooked. To test, pierce the thickest part of the fish through to the bone with a sharp knife. If the knife tip feels warm to the touch as you withdraw it, the fish is ready; if not, cook it for a little longer. Set aside to rest and cool to room temperature; the fish will continue to cook in the residual heat as it cools within its salt crust.

Use a coarse, crystally rock or sea salt but not Maldon—prized British sea salt—as it is too fine and expensive. You can buy sacks of rock salt from fishmongers or supermarkets, which shouldn't be expensive.

Meanwhile, cook the potatoes in well-salted boiling water until very tender (almost falling apart), 20 to 25 minutes. Drain and, while still warm, sprinkle with the lemon juice, season with lots of pepper, and a little more salt if necessary, and add the olive oil. Toss well to combine, then add the purslane and toss again.

To serve, crack the salt crust open with the handle of a knife or a rolling pin. Carefully remove the salt and peel off the skin from the fish. Serve the beautiful, succulent flesh warm or at room temperature, with the warm potatoes and tomato aïoli.

Squid with peppers, red wine, and wild marjoram

This beautifully colored, richly flavored stew calls for some good, open-textured peasant-style bread to mop up the juices. I also like to serve it with a generous dollop of aïoli (see page 168). I make this dish most often in early fall when bell peppers are still good, but the chill that has crept into the air calls for a depth and warmth, which the red wine and wild marjoram provide.

Serves 4 to 6

2¼ pounds small squid, with tentacles

1 tsp fennel seeds

3 cloves garlic, peeled

1 dried red chile

1 red bell pepper

1 yellow bell pepper

¼ cup mild-tasting extra virgin olive oil

2 red onions, peeled and finely sliced

few strips of orange zest

small bunch of marjoram

10 (or so) little ripe tomatoes

generous 1 cup good-quality red wine

sea salt and freshly ground black pepper

Start by cleaning the squid. Hold the body with one hand and pull out the head with the tentacles attached, using the other hand; most of the innards will come too. Cut the tentacles from the head, discarding the head. Remove the transparent quill from the body and the soft gooey matter. Rinse the body pouch and tentacles gently under cold running water, drain, and set aside in a cool place.

Toast the fennel seeds in a dry nonstick skillet over medium heat until they begin to pop and release their aroma. Meanwhile, pound the garlic using a mortar and pestle. Add the warm fennel seeds and dried chile and pound to crush and combine with the garlic. Cut the bell peppers in half lengthwise, remove the pith and seeds, then slice into 1-inch strips; set aside.

Warm 2 tbsp of the olive oil in a heavy wide pan over low heat and cook the onions gently for 10 minutes until they are soft and sweet. Add the pounded mixture, stir to combine, and cook for a couple of minutes. Now add the orange zest, sliced bell peppers, marjoram, and tomatoes.

Pour in the wine and turn up the heat slightly, so that it sizzles. Add a good pinch of salt and a grinding or two of pepper. Turn down the heat, place a lid on the pan, and cook gently for 30 minutes or so, or until the peppers are soft. You should by now have a beautifully colored stew with a deep, warm satisfying rich smell!

Heat the remaining 2 tbsp olive oil in a skillet. Season the squid generously. In batches if necessary, cook the squid in the hot pan over high heat without turning for a minute or so, then turn and cook briefly on the other side. Throw the tentacles in last of all as they take very little time to cook.

Tip the cooked squid into the hot stew and stir over the heat for a minute or so to combine the flavors. Ladle into shallow soup bowls and serve piping hot with bread.

Monkfish curry with coconut, lime, and curry leaves

I like making curries. I find it interesting and fun to build and balance the flavors—sweet, sour, salty, pungent, hot, and above all, clean and pure. Fresh curry leaves lend the most wonderful taste—just the smell of them transports me somewhere hot and exciting. Monkfish is a good choice of fish for curries and wet dishes—its firm, white, meaty flesh is a clean foil for more complex flavors.

Serves 4 to 6

1 tbsp unsalted butter or ghee

2 red onions, peeled and finely sliced

2 tsp mustard seeds

2 tsp fennel seeds

1 tsp coriander seeds

bunch of cilantro, roots and stems minced, leaves reserved

2 cloves garlic, peeled and crushed

2 fresh red chiles, chopped (seeds left in)

6 fresh curry leaves

2 kaffir lime leaves

juice of 2 limes

2 tbsp fish sauce

1 tbsp jaggery or superfine sugar

2 (12-ounce) cans good-quality peeled plum tomatoes

13/4 pounds monkfish fillet

1 (14-ounce) can coconut milk

lime wedges, to serve

Place a large heavy pan over medium-low heat. Add the butter and, once it begins to melt, add the onions. Cook over low heat for 10 minutes, stirring from time to time.

Meanwhile, toast the mustard, fennel, and coriander seeds in a dry nonstick skillet over medium heat until the spices begin to pop and release their aroma. Be careful not to burn them or they will make the curry taste bitter. Remove from the heat and, while still warm, pound to a rough powder using a mortar and pestle.

Add the ground spices to the onions along with the minced cilantro root and stems, garlic, chiles, and curry leaves. Crush the kaffir lime leaves between your fingers to help release their flavor and add to the pan. Cook for another 5 to 6 minutes... your kitchen will smell deliciously fragrant.

Add the lime juice, fish sauce, and sugar, stir once or twice, and turn up the heat slightly. Add the tomatoes and cook for 15 minutes, stirring occasionally.

Now taste the curry base. The flavor should be slightly sweet, but also sour—the spices should give a deep satisfying base note flavor; the cilantro will give it a clean light finish. Pause and consider whether all those flavors are apparent. If not, add a little more lime juice perhaps, or a little more fish sauce to underpin the flavors with a saltiness if needed. This curry base will sit happily for a day or so in the refrigerator, if you would like to make it ahead.

To finish, warm the curry over medium heat. Using a sharp knife, slice the monkfish into 1-inch pieces (it will shrink slightly during cooking). When the curry is simmering, pour in the coconut milk, stir, then add the monkfish. Cook for 3 to 4 minutes until the fish is just cooked—it will feel firm to the touch.

Scatter over the reserved cilantro leaves, ladle into bowls, and serve with lime wedges and plain rice or, as I do, with broiled flat bread laced with toasted fennel seeds.

Olive oil

Probably the single most important ingredient I use in my kitchen is extra virgin olive oil. It enhances the flavors of nearly all our vegetable dishes and salads, as well as soups and simply broiled meat and fish.

Obtained from the first pressing of the olives, extra virgin olive oil can be robust—tasting peppery, nutty, or grassy, sometimes even of hay! Other varieties can be light, fruity, and elegant. The color can range from deep murky olivey green to pale and golden, taking in all the shades in between. And the viscosity varies from light to medium; some oils are even dense and heavy. The price, too, can range from modest to wildly expensive.

You really need to try different olive oils, to find those you like the taste of and can comfortably afford. Look for labels indicating that the oil has been bottled on the estate on which the olives have been grown, hand-picked, and pressed. This is usually a sign of superior quality.

Butter has its place in cooking—lending richness and a wonderful velvety smoothness. I do use it to cook with, but more often I will reach for a bottle of olive oil. It is, of course, much better for you than butter, but as always, taste to me is the most important thing—and the flavor of good olive oil is second to none.

Olives are picked in the fall. It is only when they are properly ripe that harvesting can begin. The French claim that the "oil is in the olive" only after St. Catherine's Day on November 25; the Lebanese say that All Saints Day on November 1 marks the date. Most farmers, however, will tell you that the best time to begin harvesting is after the first rain, when the olives become easier to pick. Olives harvested early produce oil that is stronger and greener in color with the best health-giving properties, but the yield is generally lower, so many farmers prefer to wait a little longer. In my view, oils from olives picked early have the best flavor.

The finest olive oil is created when oil is extracted purely by cold pressing, with neither heat nor chemicals used in the extraction process. To be of fine quality, an oil must have less than one percent oleic acidity. Any higher percentage could mean that the oil has been extracted from damaged or badly handled fruit.

◊

We use several olive oils in the restaurant, including a lovely, slightly grassy, green oil from a small estate in Friuli in Northern Italy, as well as oils from Provence and as far away as Lebanon. Occasionally we work with some punchy oils from Spain and the very popular robust oils for which Tuscany is so famous. The one I love above all others though is the light, golden, delicate, very slightly fruity olive oil from Liguria. Made purely from a variety of olive known as *taggiasca*, it tastes wonderful and always gives me a feeling of utter contentment... making me smile.

Try different olive oils to discover your favorites. The best way to taste an olive oil is to pour a little into a glass and sip it (not directly out of your hand as is sometimes suggested). Let it roll around your tongue for a moment or two and take in the aroma from the glass. The overwhelming taste and smell, no matter how delicate, should be of the fruit from which it has been pressed.

◊

Controversially perhaps, I use good olive oil for all of my cooking both at home and at the restaurant, with the exception of deep-frying, when I use corn oil. I feel that what you cook with should always taste good straight from the bottle—it is never merely a cooking medium to me. In cases where high-temperature cooking is called for, I'll use a mild-tasting light olive oil rather than extra virgin. I tend to save the best extra virgin olive oils for dishes that I feel showcase the virtues of a full-flavored oil. And, of course, an olive oil must sit happily alongside the flavors it is paired with.

◊

As for infused olive oils, I have yet to buy one that I think tastes good. Quick to oxidize and spoil, these oils do not taste vibrant and fresh to me. I prefer to infuse my own olive oil—in small quantities for immediate use. Delicate lemon-infused oil, known as *agrumato* in Italy, is my favorite.

◊

Lemon-infused olive oil Finely pare the zest from 3 lemons in wide strips using a swivel vegetable peeler, place in a small pan, and pour over a generous 1 cup extra virgin olive oil (light in flavor, such as Ligurian). Warm gently to body temperature (around 99°F), for just 10 minutes, to release the lemon aroma. Remove from the heat and let stand for 30 minutes before using on the day of making or within 24 hours.

◊

Like all beautiful things, extra virgin olive oil should be treated with respect and care. It does not respond well to heat, light, or exposure to air, all of which cause it to oxidize. It really needs to be kept in a cool dark place—a cool pantry is perfect—and used within 6 months. I occasionally keep a small bottle by the stove but only because I know it will be used within a day or two.

Fragrant lemon-infused olive oil is lovely spooned over grilled chicken or fish, or drizzled over very fresh young sheep's or cow's milk curd.

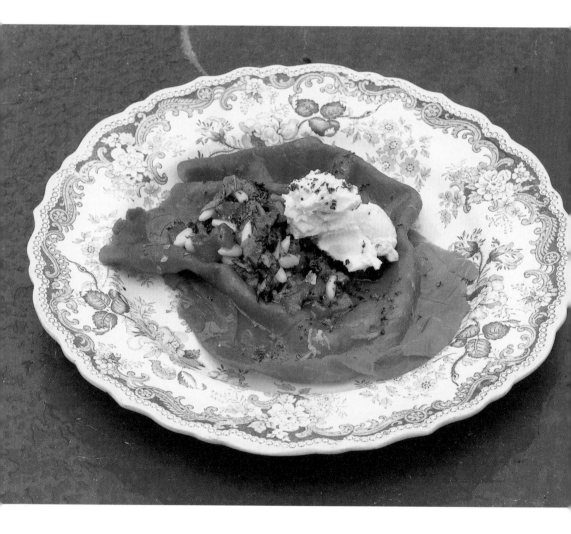

Carpaccio of beef with red pepper relish

A well-executed carpaccio makes an elegant first course. It's also a lovely way to showcase the flavor of good-quality beef. Traditionally, carpaccio is simply finely sliced pounded beef, dressed with nothing more than salt, extra virgin olive oil, and perhaps a few shavings of Parmesan. Here, I have paired it with a little more—summery red bell peppers and the lightest curd cheese. In winter we serve it with shavings of white truffle, deep-fried artichoke hearts, or slivers of white celery heart.

Serves 4 or 8

1 pound 2 ounces beef tenderloin, sinew or fat trimmed off

extra virgin olive oil, to drizzle

sea salt

juice of 1/2 lemon, or to taste

Red pepper relish

1 large red bell pepper

1/4 cup currants

1/3 cup pine nuts

sea salt and freshly ground black pepper

1 small clove garlic, peeled and minced

small bunch of basil, leaves only, minced

small bunch of arugula, chopped

4 tsp sherry vinegar

1 tsp Pedro Ximénez sherry

1/4 cup mild-tasting extra virgin olive oil

To serve

4 generous tbsp fromage blanc or other sweet young curd cheese

Wrap the meat and place in the freezer for 20 to 30 minutes until thoroughly chilled but not frozen. (This makes it easier to slice.)

Cut sixteen 10-inch squares of parchment paper. Using a very sharp knife, slice the meat with the grain into 8 slices. Brush one parchment square with a little olive oil and lay a slice of meat on top. Cover with a second oiled square of parchment. Working from the center outward, pound the meat evenly and gently using a wooden rolling pin. Keep pounding (but not too hard or you will tear the flesh) until the meat is no more than 1/8 inch thick. When you have finished, the slice should be two or three times its original size. Continue until you have 8 slices of finished carpaccio. Refrigerate until ready to serve, but for no longer than 4 hours, or the meat will discolor and lose flavor.

To make the relish, roast the pepper under a hot broiler, turning until the skin is charred all over. Transfer to a bowl, cover, and let stand for 20 minutes. Preheat the oven to 375°F (convection oven to 350°F). Soak the currants in a little warm water for 15 minutes to soften. Warm the pine nuts in the oven for just a few minutes to release their flavor.

Peel, halve, and seed the bell pepper, then cut into small dice and place in a bowl. Add the pine nuts. Squeeze out the excess water from the currants and add these. Season with salt and pepper and add the garlic, basil, arugula, vinegar, sherry, and olive oil. Stir well and let stand for a few minutes, then taste and adjust the seasoning. The relish should be slightly sweet, soft, and fresh.

To assemble, carefully peel off one sheet of parchment paper from each package. Then lay a slice, exposed side down, on each chilled plate and peel off the top layer of paper. Add a second slice of beef to each plate if serving two each. Drizzle with the olive oil, season with salt, and sprinkle with a few drops of lemon juice. Spoon over the relish, leaving most of the meat exposed. Finish with the fromage blanc and a final drizzle of relish. Serve immediately.

Ribollita

You will, no doubt, have seen this soup documented many times before. A much-loved dish from Tuscany, it consists of little more than reboiled beans, tomatoes, stale bread, and cavolo nero—the beautiful black leaf kale that hails from the region. My version replaces the bread with farro, but holds the tradition of finishing with lashings of beautiful peppery, grassy Tuscan oil. I often make this soup at home for my children—we let it sit on top of the stove and dip into it as we feel like it. To me this is ultimate comfort food ... good for you in the extreme.

Serves 6 to 8

2 cups dried cannellini beans, soaked in cold water overnight

about 3 quarts water

3 tbsp olive oil

2 onions, peeled and chopped

1 dried red chile, crumbled

sea salt and freshly ground black pepper

2 celery stalks, chopped

2 carrots, peeled and chopped

3 small cloves garlic, peeled and smashed

small bunch of sage

2 potatoes, peeled and chopped

5 ounces farro, well rinsed under cold water

1 (14-ounce) can good-quality peeled plum tomatoes

bunch of cavolo nero, thick stalks removed, roughly chopped

extra virgin olive oil, preferably Tuscan, to serve

Drain the beans and place them in a heavy pan. Pour over about 2 quarts water to cover generously and cook over low heat until the beans are soft, about 1½ hours. Drain and set aside.

Heat the olive oil in a separate pot (large enough to hold all the ingredients comfortably) over low heat. Add the onions, chile, and a pinch of salt. Sweat gently until the onions are soft and translucent.

Add the celery, carrots, garlic, sage, potatoes, and farro. Cook for a couple of minutes to allow the heat to begin to release the flavors of the vegetables, then add the tomatoes. Cover and simmer over low heat for 20 minutes.

Stir in the cooked beans, then cover with about 1 quart water—just enough for a thick brothy base in which the vegetables can cook properly. Add the cavolo nero and reduce the heat to low. Cover and cook for another hour until the vegetables are really soft. Add a pinch of salt and a few good grindings of black pepper.

Remove from the heat and let cool completely. Let the ribollita stand for a couple of hours—this will improve the flavor immensely!

To serve, reheat the soup. Taste and adjust the seasoning if necessary, then drizzle generously with extra virgin olive oil. Turn up the heat to emulsify, then ladle into warm bowls.

Slow-cooked dishes more often than not taste better if they are removed from the stove once they are cooked and allowed to settle to room temperature, then reheated to serve. Also, these dishes call for patience from the start. Slow, gentle cooking of onions, chile, garlic, or whatever else the recipe asks you to lay down will give a much better flavor than if you rush it. Gentle, respectful cooking results in a dish that is sweeter, richer, and far more complex.

Wild sea bass with salmoriglio

Salmoriglio is a pungent marinade-cum-sauce from Sicily. It is traditionally made with oregano though I generally use marjoram, as we have a profusion in our vegetable garden during the summer. You can make the sauce a few days in advance—leaving the flavors to mature and intensify at room temperature (not in the refrigerator)—but add the lemon juice just before you are ready to use it. In the summer, I often serve this fish dish simply with sliced perfectly ripe tomatoes, drizzled with olive oil, and really good, chewy peasant-style bread.

Serves 4

4 wild sea bass fillets (with skin), about 6¹⁄₂ ounces each

1 tbsp olive oil

sea salt and freshly ground black pepper

lemon wedges, to serve

Salmoriglio

4 small cloves garlic, peeled and roughly sliced

¹⁄₂ tsp good-quality sea salt

¹⁄₂ tsp dried red chile flakes

bunch of marjoram or oregano, leaves only

scant 1 cup extra virgin olive oil

¹⁄₂ lemon

First make the salmoriglio. Pound the garlic using a mortar and pestle to a rough paste, then add the salt and continue to pound until smooth. Add the chile and marjoram and pound lightly, then pour in the olive oil and stir well to combine. If using straightaway, squeeze over the lemon juice; otherwise, set aside, adding the lemon juice just before serving.

To cook the fish, preheat the broiler. On the skin side only, brush with olive oil and season generously with salt and pepper. Lay the fish, flesh side down, on the broiler rack and place under the heat.

Cook the sea bass fillets without turning for 5 to 6 minutes, or until the skin is blistered and deliciously crisp and the flesh underneath is delicately translucent.

Carefully transfer the fish fillets, skin side up, to warm plates and spoon over the salmoriglio. Serve at once, with lemon wedges, good bread or new potatoes, and a salad.

Salmoriglio is an excellent marinade for chicken or lamb, and is perfect for basting fish and red meat during cooking. Or you can simply spoon it over cooked fish (as here), meat, or vegetables before serving. It is particularly good smeared over broiled eggplants or roasted squash, or drizzled over ripe tomatoes.

Leaves

I have often thought that my very last meal on this earth would have to be some sort of salad. Other things would certainly be involved, but it would be composed primarily of leaves, dressed with a beautiful extra virgin olive oil and a touch of acidity. I eat salad every day—I never tire of it as I find the possible flavor combinations endless.

When I grew up in Australia, the choice of salad leaves was limited—to crunchy, watery iceberg; crisp romaine; and a few other lettuces, but little else. Arugula, radicchio, corn salad, and frisée were unheard of, and it wasn't until I moved to Europe in my early twenties that I was able to sample all the beautiful loose-leafed and tightly spun varieties from France, Italy, and elsewhere. I love them all, but arugula, purslane, and baby spinach feature strongly in my dishes. And my favorite family of leaves encompasses dandelion and the raddichio family—treviso, Castelfranco, tardivo—all of which are elegant to behold and bittersweet to taste.

Almost everything I serve at the restaurant or at home arrives with a tangle of one leaf or another. Sometimes, when the leaves are perfect, I'll present just one variety on its own—choosing it carefully to complement the food it is to be served with. At other times, a variety of leaves is called for—some sweet, some bitter, some with bite, some soft—often with a handful of herb leaves thrown in.

◊

We grow lots of young, sweet leaves in the summer, including purslane, lollo rosso, mizuna, mignonette, pea shoots, and arugula, which has a strength of flavor that I love. Arugula thrives easily, and with each cutting, it grows back stronger—and seemingly more intensely flavored. I urge you to try and grow some, even if you only have a pot or window box. I'm also very fond of purslane—both the summer and winter varieties. Succulent and bouncy, it adds a fresh clean bite to salads. Pea shoots lend a similar vibrancy—totally delicious, they taste more of sweet fresh peas than the vegetables do themselves.

Some of the most interesting leaves—including the endives, red-leafed tardivo, treviso, radicchio, and Castelfranco (shown on pages 84 to 85), and dandelion (shown left)—are winter leaves. Some are attractively speckled, others striped, but all have a languid beauty that is truly breathtaking. Their distinctive bitter taste counterbalances rich winter dishes perfectly.

◊

Do try to grow some of your own leaves, or at least source more exciting varieties from farmers' markets and good greengrocers. Obviously, all leaves are best used as soon as possible after picking or buying. If you need to store them for a day or two, keep them loosely covered with a damp dish towel in the produce drawer of the refrigerator, but handle carefully, for they are fragile and suffer refrigerator burn and bruising easily.

All things must be considered when composing a salad—texture and flavor of course, but also the color and shape of the various leaves.

Wash salad leaves gently and only if they really need it. Gently pat them dry with a clean dish towel or invest in a good salad spinner. This is essential, for leaves that are water sodden will be heavy and disappointing—and the dressing will taste diluted and slip from the leaves rather than cling to them.

◊

Like all things, leaves have their season and none is available all year round. The winter months are filled with the bitter leaves, whereas in summer we have the softer fresher varieties. There is, however, something to enjoy every month throughout the year.

Middle Eastern salad of cucumber, lettuce, and herbs

I love the idea of this salad. When I was a child, my father, who rarely ever cooked, would sometimes prepare a chopped salad that he had eaten in America. It comprised several ingredients—often crunchy lettuce, sweet tomatoes, and cheese or some form of meat—chopped into small pieces and tossed with a good dressing. This is more a Middle East version, without meat or cheese. It is almost the consistency of gazpacho, but laced with plenty of cool, crunchy romaine lettuce.

Serves 4

2 very ripe tomatoes

1 small cucumber

1 red onion, peeled and minced

1 red bell pepper, cored, seeded, and chopped

6 radishes, chopped

1 fresh red chile, seeded and minced

bunch of Italian parsley, leaves only, chopped

bunch of mint, leaves only, chopped

small bunch of dill, leaves only, minced

1/2 tsp dried mint

1 tsp red wine vinegar

juice of 1/2 lemon

1/2 tsp pomegranate molasses

sea salt

3 tbsp extra virgin olive oil

1 pomegranate

1 small head tender romaine lettuce

Chop the tomatoes into small dice and place in a large bowl. Halve the cucumber lengthwise and scoop out the seeds, then cut into pieces the same size as the tomatoes and add to the bowl. Add the onion, bell pepper, radishes, chile, fresh herbs, and dried mint. Stir well to combine.

In a separate bowl, combine the vinegar, lemon juice, molasses, a good pinch of salt, and the olive oil. Stir well and pour over the chopped vegetables. Toss gently and let macerate for 10 minutes.

Hold the pomegranate in one hand and gently tap it all over with a rolling pin to loosen the seeds. Now cut the fruit in half and extract the seeds with your fingers—do this over a bowl to catch them and any juice. Pick out any strands of bitter pith that have dropped into the bowl.

Just before serving, shred the lettuce and toss with the salad. Taste and season with a little more salt if necessary. Pile onto a serving plate and sprinkle with the pomegranate seeds. Serve with warm flat bread or as an accompaniment to simple broiled fish.

Pink grapefruit, avocado, and watercress salad

This elegant, light salad is ideal to serve as a first course. Pink grapefruit and peppery watercress cut the richness of avocado, and a scattering of toasted hazelnuts and hazelnut oil in the dressing suggest a flavor of early fall. Prosciutto is a graceful inclusion, but you can leave it out for a lighter vegetarian salad if you like.

Serves 4

16 shelled hazelnuts

bunch of watercress

1 pink grapefruit

1 ripe avocado

8 to 12 slices of prosciutto

8 to 12 wafer-thin slices of young romano (optional)

1 tbsp minced parsley

Dressing

1 tbsp Dijon mustard

2 tbsp sherry vinegar

sea salt and freshly ground black pepper

3 tbsp mild-tasting extra virgin olive oil

3 tbsp hazelnut oil

First make the dressing. Combine the mustard and vinegar in a bowl and add a pinch each of salt and pepper. Whisk in the olive oil, followed by the hazelnut oil to emulsify, then set aside.

Preheat the oven to 375°F (convection oven to 350°F). Place the nuts on a baking sheet and roast in the middle of the oven for 2 to 4 minutes to warm and release their flavor. Place in a clean cloth and rub gently to remove the skins, then roughly chop the nuts.

For the salad, wash the watercress and gently pat dry. Peel the grapefruit, removing all the pith and seeds, then cut out the segments over a large bowl to catch the juice as well as the segments. Halve, pit, and peel the avocado, then cut into slices, similar in size to the grapefruit. Add to the grapefruit with the watercress and toss gently with your fingers to mix.

If the dressing has separated on standing, give it a whisk, then drizzle half of it over the salad and toss lightly, so you don't break up the avocado or grapefruit. Taste and adjust the seasoning.

Arrange the salad on plates, interleaving the prosciutto slices and romano with the watercress, grapefruit, and avocado. Sprinkle with the minced parsley and drizzle over the remaining dressing. Finally, scatter over the hazelnuts and serve.

Roasted vegetable salad with arugula and tomatoes

Deeply colorful, sweet, and warm, this is a favorite salad of mine. We make it with arugula and beet from our garden—I also like to throw in the beet tops, which make the most delicious salad leaf. Don't drown this beautiful salad with dressing—you want to allow all the colors and earthy sweet flavors to shine through.

Serves 4

12 small young beets, with leafy tops

1 small red onion, peeled and sliced into pinwheels

1/4 cup olive oil

sea salt and freshly ground black pepper

1 tbsp balsamic vinegar

1 large (or 2 medium) sweet potato

1/2 tbsp maple syrup

1/2 tbsp tamari or soy sauce

1 dried red chile, crumbled

juice of 1/2 lime

2 small fennel bulbs, trimmed

12 little ripe tomatoes

large handful of arugula leaves

extra virgin olive oil, to drizzle

Dressing

generous 3/4 cup thick strained plain yogurt

10 drops of Tabasco

juice of 1/2 lime

3 tbsp extra virgin olive oil

sea salt

small bunch of cilantro, leaves only

First make the dressing. Put the yogurt in a bowl and stir in the Tabasco, most of the lime juice, the olive oil, and a pinch of salt. Mince the cilantro and stir into the dressing. Taste and add a little more salt or lime juice if needed. Set aside.

Preheat the oven to 425°F (convection oven to 400°F). Scrub the beets well under cold running water to remove any dirt, but don't bother to peel them. Cut off the tops, wash these, pat them dry, and set aside for later.

Put the beets and onion rings in a roasting pan, pour over 2 tbsp olive oil, and season with salt and pepper. Cover tightly with foil and roast in the oven until the beets are tender when pierced with a sharp knife, 30 to 40 minutes. Take out the onion rings and set aside. Return the beets to the oven and bake, uncovered, for another 10 to 15 minutes until the skins are crinkly. Place in a bowl and dress, while warm, with the balsamic vinegar. Set aside to cool.

Meanwhile, peel the sweet potato and cut into 1 1/2-inch chunks. Place in a bowl and spoon over the maple syrup, tamari, and 1 tbsp olive oil. Toss to coat, then place in a roasting pan and scatter over the chile. Roast, uncovered, on the middle shelf of the oven until tender when pierced with a knife, 25 to 35 minutes. Remove and, while warm, sprinkle over the lime juice. Let cool.

Quarter the fennel bulbs and place in a roasting pan. Season with salt and pepper and drizzle with 1 tbsp olive oil. Cover with foil and bake in the oven for 20 minutes, then remove the foil and throw in the tomatoes. Return to the oven and cook, uncovered, until the fennel is soft and the tomatoes are soft and oozing their juice, 10 to 20 minutes. Remove and let cool.

Put the arugula and the beet tops in a bowl, dress with a little extra virgin olive oil, and season lightly. Arrange the salad on individual plates, layering the leaves and roasted vegetables, and spooning over a little dressing here and there as you go. Serve at once.

Salad of summer leaves and flowers

When combining different leaves to make a salad, it is important to consider flavor, but also texture and color. I like to include bitter as well as sweet leaves, choosing some that are watery and crunchy, others that are soft and succulent. A peppery note of watercress or arugula is a good addition, too. Among my other favorites are baby spinach and chard, purslane, pea shoots, romaine, escarole, corn salad, and the slightly bitter members of the *chicoria* family. Sometimes we add flowers to our salads, which not only look beautiful, but also have their own distinctive flavors. My preferred dressing for leaves is simply olive oil and lemon juice.

Serves 4

selection of different leaves (see above)

handful of soft herb leaves (chervil, Italian parsley, basil, etc.)

handful of edible flowers (nasturtiums, violets, pansies, borage, and/or other herb flowers), optional

Dressing

juice of 1/2 lemon, or to taste

generous 1/3 cup mild-tasting extra virgin olive oil

sea salt and freshly ground black pepper

For the dressing, whisk the lemon juice and olive oil together to combine, seasoning with salt and pepper to taste. Seasoning is very important—salt really makes leaves come alive.

If necessary, wash the salad and herb leaves and gently pat dry. Place in a large bowl and toss with a little of the dressing. Scatter over the flowers to serve.

Keep any leftover dressing in a screw-topped jar and use within a day or two, shaking it well to re-emulsify.

Always dress leaves using your fingertips—a light touch is imperative—but you also need to be quite thorough. An underdressed salad is very disappointing to eat. Equally, don't overdo it, as too much oil or vinaigrette will overpower the delicate flavors of the leaves.

Langoustines with cooked spinach, purple basil, and tomato aïoli

I love this combination of earthy, inky green leaves and sweet, succulent langoustines—or Dublin Bay prawns as they are also known. The tomato aïoli brings the flavors together perfectly. If you cannot get langoustines, you'll find the dish also works beautifully with shrimp or scallops.

Serves 4

about 24 live langoustines (6 per person)

sea salt and freshly ground black pepper

3 tbsp extra virgin olive oil

juice of 1/2 lemon

10 ounces spinach

grated zest of 1 lemon

bunch of purple basil, leaves only

Fresh tomato aïoli

3 little ripe plum tomatoes

3 organic egg yolks

1/2 tsp Dijon mustard

2 cloves garlic, peeled and crushed

juice of 1 lemon

sea salt and freshly ground black pepper

generous 1 cup extra virgin olive oil

Ask your fishmonger for live langoustines and keep them in a box covered with damp newspaper until ready to cook.

Start by making the aïoli. Preheat the oven to 425°F (convection oven to 400°F). Pierce each tomato once with a small sharp knife and place in a small roasting pan. Roast on the middle shelf of the oven until the tomatoes are soft and their skins have split slightly, 10 to 15 minutes. Set aside to cool.

Place the egg yolks in a food processor and add the mustard, garlic, lemon juice, and the cooled tomatoes. Add a pinch of salt and a little pepper. Whiz briefly to combine. Now, with the motor running, slowly add the olive oil in a fine stream until it is all incorporated and the aïoli is emulsified. Taste and adjust the seasoning.

For the langoustines, place a large pot of water on to boil and salt it generously. When it reaches a rolling boil, drop in the langoustines and cook for 3 minutes. Remove and let cool. When cool enough to handle, peel the langoustines, removing the flesh in one piece. Season with salt and pepper and dress with a little of the olive oil. Sprinkle with a few drops of lemon juice.

Wash the spinach in several changes of cold water to ensure that no dirt is clinging to the leaves. Warm a medium heavy pan over medium heat. Add the spinach, in batches if necessary, with just the water clinging to the leaves. This alone will create steam and allow the spinach to quickly wilt. Once wilted, tip it into a colander and let cool. When cool, squeeze the spinach between the palms of your hands to remove as much moisture as possible. Dress with the remaining olive oil, the lemon zest, and juice. Season with salt and pepper.

To assemble the salad, place the spinach in a bowl with the basil and langoustines. Toss together gently to combine. Arrange on individual serving plates and spoon a little of the aïoli over the top.

Salad of poached salmon, black rice, and watercress

For the best possible flavor, you would need to poach a whole salmon, but given the size this is often impractical—you'll most probably find it more convenient to poach fillets. Choose wild salmon though, as the flavor is far superior and more delicate. Watercress is a natural partner for salmon, as its slightly peppery leaves balance the sweet flavor of the flesh. If black rice is difficult to locate, you'll find cooked cannellini beans are equally delicious.

Serves 6

2¹/4 pounds wild salmon

2 carrots, peeled and chopped

2 celery stalks, chopped

small bunch of tarragon

3 bay leaves

6 black peppercorns

1/3 cup black rice

salt and freshly ground black pepper

1/4 cup extra virgin olive oil

juice of 1 lime

bunch of watercress

Dressing

2 ripe tomatoes, chopped

1 tbsp freshly grated horseradish

finely grated zest and juice of 1 lime

2 tbsp olive oil

1/2 cup crème fraîche

sea salt

To finish

small handful of chervil leaves, minced

Place the salmon in a wide, shallow pan with the carrots, celery, tarragon, bay leaves, and peppercorns. Pour over sufficient water to cover and bring to a bare simmer over medium heat. As soon as the water reaches a simmer, turn off the heat and let the fish cook in the residual heat of the poaching liquor as it cools.

Cook the black rice in boiling salted water according to the package directions until al dente; it will take 35 to 40 minutes.

Mix 2 tbsp olive oil with the lime juice and some salt and pepper. When the salmon is cool, remove it from the liquor to a plate and brush with the lime and oil mixture. Set aside.

To make the dressing, put the tomatoes into a bowl and stir in the horseradish, lime zest and juice, olive oil, and crème fraîche. Season with a good pinch of salt.

To assemble the salad, wash the watercress and pat dry, then place in a bowl and dress with 1 tbsp olive oil and a small pinch of salt. Dress the rice in a separate bowl, also with 1 tbsp olive oil and a little salt. Remove the skin from the salmon and gently flake into pieces, using your fingers.

Arrange the watercress, rice, and salmon on individual plates, layering them attractively. Drizzle over the dressing and sprinkle with the chervil to serve.

Citrus

When I started following the rhythm of the seasons in my cooking, I was so surprised to learn that citrus were primarily winter fruits. To me, they speak so absolutely of summer, of sunshine, and warmth. Their powerful burst of flavor suggests a product of blue skies, long days, and, most importantly, heat. Now I realize that nature's majesty has bestowed these jewels during the winter months to give a sense of sustenance and hope, such is the perfection of the natural world.

Intense and beautiful in color, with clear, clean, top note flavors, they are a real gift and offer such diversity. Tarocco blood oranges, Seville oranges, kumquats, clementines, mandarins, pink grapefruit, citrons, lemons, and limes are among the citrus fruit that I love to cook with. In truth, I would find it almost impossible to work without citrus fruits—their flavors are as necessary to my cooking as the use of salt.

Many citrus trees can, in fact, bear fruit for most of the year, though they blossom and fruit most notably in late December and January. Some not-to-be-missed varieties, however—including clementines, Seville oranges, mandarins, and blood oranges—have a short season, lasting only two or three months during the winter or spring. Most of our citrus fruit comes from Italy, Spain, and North Africa, though at Petersham we are fortunate to have a number of trees, including lemon, kaffir lime, Meyer lemon, and kumquat. To be able to walk into a greenhouse and pluck lemons and other citrus fruit from the tree through the year is a real treat, not least because the trees themselves are visually so beautiful.

◊

When you are buying citrus fruit, choose fruit that feels heavy for its size. Avoid any with bruises, but don't worry about blemishes, as these occur naturally during ripening. Buy organic fruit if possible, and scrub well before use.

◊

Lemon juice is the ingredient, along with salt, that I depend on more than anything in the kitchen. It makes food come alive and I use the sharp juice to flavor so many dishes. Never is there a day when my kitchen is without a bowl of lemons.

All citrus fruits have intensely flavored zest and juice, which give a zing to dishes—sweet and savory. I use freshly squeezed lemon juice in so many ways—to make lemonade; dress vegetables and salads; drizzle over fish; cut the richness of mayonnaise made with extra virgin olive oil, and so on. I add the peel to slow-cooked dishes to impart vibrancy and life, and I strew the grated zest on almost everything—to add freshness and high notes.

Blood oranges, at their peak in January and February, are one of my favorites. I use them to make jellies and other palate-cleansing desserts. Their juice also lends a vibrancy to savory dishes—try it in an aïoli to serve with roasted sea bass or deep-fried artichokes. Warm and intense, this garlicky mayonnaise with a hint of citrus is a beautiful pale orangey-red color.

In January, we make big vats of marmalade from the bitter juice and skin of Seville oranges to sell in the store at Petersham; we also eat it on sourdough toast cooked under the broiler to take the chill off the early mornings.

We pickle limes to make a sour relish, which is perfect with dishes that are spice laden and Indian in spirit. We also preserve lemons in salt—to chop and add to veal stews, or slow-cooked dishes that are Middle Eastern in feel. Their peculiar and pungent taste is unique.

And we candy everything we possibly can, especially citron peel and pinwheels of clementines and blood oranges. To my mind, nothing works better with bitter chocolate than candied orange peel.

Lemonade

Week in, week out, we make this mouthwateringly sharp, refreshing drink—just as we did when the restaurant first opened without a license to sell alcohol. When I see a full pitcher of freshly made lemonade, crammed with crushed ice and fresh mint, it still makes me smile. It reflects most truly our roots and our ethos.

Makes about 8 cups

8 lemons

1 cup superfine sugar

6^1/$_3$ to 8 cups sparkling water, to dilute

mint sprigs, to serve

Squeeze the juice from the lemons and pour into a pan. Add the sugar and stir well. Place over medium heat and bring to a simmer, stirring occasionally to dissolve the sugar. Cook gently for 5 to 6 minutes, then remove from the heat. Pour into a pitcher and cool.

When completely cool, cover and place in the refrigerator. This lemonade base keeps well, though you'll probably use it all within a few days.

To serve, pour some lemonade base into a pitcher—to fill it by about a quarter. Add plenty of ice and top off with sparkling water to taste. Add a handful of mint sprigs and serve.

Lemon and orange curd

Sharp, yet sweet and comforting, this is a really satisfying thing to make. Old-fashioned in a way, it has a deep, nostalgic flavor, triggering memories—flavors that achieve this are particularly special to me. You can vary the taste by adding the juice of other citrus fruit, like blood oranges, as I have here. But don't be tempted to omit the lemon altogether as its acidity is needed to prevent the curd from becoming overly sweet.

Makes about 1 pound 2 ounces

finely grated zest and juice of 2 lemons

finely grated zest and juice of 1 blood orange

3/4 cup superfine sugar

6 organic egg yolks

generous 3/4 cup unsalted butter, cut into small pieces

Mix the lemon and orange zests and juice, sugar, and egg yolks together in a heatproof bowl until well combined. Stand the bowl over a pan of simmering water (or simply pour the mixture straight into a medium heavy pan and place over very low heat if you are confident that you can keep the direct heat low enough).

Stir continuously with a wooden spoon as the mixture begins to warm and gradually thicken. Don't let it boil or it will curdle. Once the curd is thick enough to coat the back of the spoon, 7 to 10 minutes, remove from the heat.

Immediately stir in the butter, piece by piece. Strain the curd through a fine strainer into a clean bowl or a warm sterilized jar. Cover or seal and store in the refrigerator. It will keep for a good week or so.

Deep-fried artichokes and lemon with mint and anchovy dressing

I like to deep-fry things in the manner of Italian *fritto misto*—it is a lovely informal way of mixing and matching ingredients. Over the years, I have deep-fried almost everything, from little anchovies to soft ripe figs! A good accompanying sauce is essential. This sharp, salty dressing is a perfect foil for crispy battered artichokes—try serving it with other deep-fried vegetables, too.

Serves 4

12 small, tender artichokes

juice of 1 lemon (if preparing ahead)

2 lemons

corn oil, to deep-fry

Batter

23/4 cups all-purpose flour

sea salt

1/2 cup olive oil

scant 1/3 cup sparkling water

1 organic egg white

Mint and anchovy dressing

5 good-quality anchovy fillets, packed in salt or olive oil

bunch of mint, leaves only

2 to 21/2 tbsp red wine vinegar

1/2 cup extra virgin olive oil

You'll have more batter than you need here, but it keeps well in the refrigerator and is perfect for a *piccolo fritto* of lovage leaves. Simply draw the leaves through the batter and deep-fry until crisp and golden. Use as a garnish for meat or fish.

First make the batter. Sift the flour into a bowl, add a pinch of salt, and make a well in the middle. Pour in the olive oil, whisking well to combine, then whisk in the sparkling water. In another bowl, whisk the egg white to firm peaks, then fold into the batter. (You can make this batter a few hours ahead.)

For the dressing, rinse the anchovies well if they are packed in salt, then drain and pat dry. Place the anchovies in a blender, along with the mint leaves and 2 tbsp vinegar. With the motor running, slowly pour in the olive oil through the feeder tube until it is all incorporated. Taste and add a little more wine vinegar if you like; you shouldn't need any salt.

To prepare the artichokes, trim away the darker tough outer leaves with a sharp knife and trim and peel the stem. Cut off the tops of the artichoke leaves at the point where their color becomes darker. Now cut each artichoke in half lengthwise and remove the hairy choke. If not using immediately, immerse in a bowl of water acidulated with the lemon juice to prevent them from discoloring. Slice the lemons into fairly thin circles (but not so thin that they will fall apart when deep-fried).

When ready to cook, drain the artichokes and pat dry. Heat the corn oil in a deep-fryer or other suitable heavy pan to 350°F, or until a cube of bread dropped in sizzles and browns quickly. You'll need to cook the artichokes in batches. Dip in the batter and turn to coat, then lift out letting the excess batter fall off. Deep-fry three or four at a time for about 11/2 minutes until golden and tender. Remove and drain on paper towels; keep hot while you cook the rest. Deep-fry the lemon slices in the same way—don't overcrowd the pan or they will stick together. When golden, remove and drain.

Serve the crispy artichokes and lemon slices on warm plates drizzled with the mint and anchovy dressing. I like to serve a simply dressed arugula salad alongside, for a nice clean contrast.

Broiled poussins with lemon, marjoram, flat bread, and garlicky yogurt

We cooked this in a wood-fired oven one beautiful, warm summer's evening. The combination of tender chicken, garlicky yogurt, and sweet summer tomatoes—mopped up with the thinnest possible bread—was truly memorable. It helped that the poussins were salted beforehand, which makes their flesh really tender and flavorful. You might not be able to create quite the same effect without a wood-fired oven, but it will taste delicious all the same.

Serves 4

4 poussins, butterflied with backbone removed and flattened

1 tbsp coarse sea salt

juice of 1 lemon

small bunch of marjoram, leaves only, chopped

1 fresh red chile, finely sliced

1/4 cup extra virgin olive oil

Yogurt dressing

1 1/4 cup thick strained plain yogurt

2 cloves garlic, peeled and crushed

pinch of sea salt

3 tbsp extra virgin olive oil

To serve

4 Arab-style flat breads or pita breads

about 12 cherry tomatoes, halved

large handful of wild arugula

few marjoram leaves, roughly torn

A day ahead, lay the butterflied poussins on a board and sprinkle evenly all over with the coarse salt. Cover with a clean cloth and place in the refrigerator.

The next day, an hour or so before you are ready to cook, take the poussins out of the refrigerator and let them return to room temperature. Brush off any excess salt and do not reseason. Sprinkle with the lemon juice. Stir the marjoram and chile into the olive oil, then rub this mixture all over the birds and set aside.

To make the yogurt dressing, put the yogurt into a bowl and add the garlic, salt, and olive oil. Stir well, then taste and adjust the seasoning if necessary.

When ready to cook, heat up your broiler or grill. When it is really hot, lay the poussins, skin side down, on the rack and cook for 6 to 8 minutes. Then turn and cook for another 8 minutes on the other side. The skin should be golden and blistered in some places, the flesh underneath meltingly tender. A minute or two before the poussins will be ready, add the flat breads to the broiler to warm through, turning once.

Arrange the poussins on warm plates, with the warm breads, tomatoes, and arugula. Spoon over the yogurt dressing and scatter over a little marjoram to serve.

Clementines with Medjool dates, pomegranates, and honeyed almonds

This is a very simple, fruity winter dessert, based on a handful of ingredients that are in season, are at their best, and go together beautifully. Like all simple things, it relies on good produce, prepared thoughtfully and as close to eating as is possible. I use the majestic Medjool dates, which lend a lovely caramely taste. And the honey I like to use is chestnut—dark in color, with a slightly bitter, molasses flavor.

Serves 4

scant 1/3 cup chestnut honey (or other fragrant honey)

20 blanched almonds

1 pomegranate

4 clementines

6 Medjool dates

4 rounded tbsp mascarpone

Put the honey into a pan and bring to a simmer over medium heat. Add the almonds and stir once or twice to coat them in the honey. Cook for a couple of minutes, then remove from the heat and set aside.

Now you need to extract the seeds from the pomegranate. I find the easiest way to do this is by holding the pomegranate in one hand and gently tapping it all over with a wooden rolling pin, moving the pomegranate as I tap it. This loosens the teardrop-shaped seeds from the bitter white pith that clings to them. Cut the fruit in half—the seeds should now be easy for you to remove with your fingers. Do this over a bowl to catch any juice. When you've finished, pick out any strands of bitter membrane that might have dropped into the bowl.

Using a small sharp knife, slice off both ends of the clementines, then cut away the peel and pith, following the contour of the fruit. Now cut the segments free, catching the juice and adding it to the pomegranate seeds as you do so. Cut each date into 5 or 6 slices, discarding the seeds.

To assemble, arrange the clementine segments on large individual plates. Scatter over the dates, pomegranate seeds, and juice, placing a spoonful of mascarpone in the center. Scatter over the honeyed almonds and serve.

Blood oranges with warm honey and rosemary

This is one of my all-time favorite desserts. I love its utter simplicity and purity of flavor. It is the perfect way to round off one of those slow-cooked slightly heavier meals that we are drawn to during the colder months. As a soaring clean palate-cleanser, it leaves you feeling lighter and refreshed at the end.

Serves 4

6 blood oranges

generous ½ cup light, fragrant honey

3 tbsp water

3 to 4 rosemary sprigs, plus extra sprigs to garnish

1 small dried red chile, seeded and very finely sliced (optional)

To prepare the oranges, using a small sharp knife, slice off both ends, then stand them upright on a board. Running the knife from the top to the bottom, cut away the peel and pith, following the contour of the fruit. Now slice the oranges across into pinwheels— I usually get 5 slices from each orange. Remove the seeds. Set the slices aside while you warm the honey.

Put the honey and water into a small pan. Lay the rosemary on a wooden cutting board and using a rolling pin, gently pound the stalk and leaves to bruise them and release their flavor. Add the rosemary to the pan and place over very low heat. Allow the honey to warm through very gently for a few minutes, stirring from time to time; don't let the mixture boil. Remove from the heat and set aside to infuse for 10 minutes, then remove the rosemary.

To serve, arrange the orange pinwheels on individual plates. Sprinkle with the dried chile and spoon over the infused honey. Scatter over a few fresh rosemary sprigs and serve.

Pink grapefruit and sherry sherbet

This icy-cold dessert is so light it is almost ethereal. The addition of Pedro Ximénez—a dark, rich raisin-flavored sweet sherry—underpins the sherbet. You can use blood orange, clementine, or mandarin juice rather than pink grapefruit if you prefer—all of these have distinctive flavors and work well here. You'll need approximately 2 1/2 cups juice.

Serves 4

6 pink grapefruit
3/4 cup superfine sugar
generous 3/4 cup heavy cream
1 vanilla bean, split lengthwise
3 tbsp Pedro Ximénez sherry

Cut the grapefruit in half and squeeze to extract as much juice from them as possible. Strain the juice through a colander into a bowl and set aside.

Put the sugar and cream into a small heavy pan. Scrape the seeds from the vanilla bean and add them to the pan together with the empty bean. Place over medium heat and bring just to a boil, stirring once or twice to dissolve the sugar. Lower the heat and simmer gently for a minute or so—you simply want to infuse the cream with the flavor of vanilla. Remove and set aside to cool.

Once the infused cream is cool, pour it through a strainer onto the grapefruit juice and stir well, then add the sherry. Pour the mixture into an ice-cream maker and churn until thickened, following the manufacturer's instructions.

Spoon into chilled bowls and serve the sherbet just as it is to fully appreciate its refreshing taste and wonderful texture.

Ices and sorbets need to have a strong, distinguishing taste before they are frozen. Chilling dulls flavor, so they will taste more subtle once frozen.

Chocolate-dipped candied citrons and clementines

Candied orange peel dipped in chocolate was one of my favorite things when I was young. My mother would serve these bittersweet treats with coffee at the end of a dinner party and I thought they were the most glamorous things in the world! I still love the taste. We make these around Christmas to serve with coffee in the restaurant. The candied fruit, before dipping, can be wrapped and kept in the refrigerator for up to 4 months to be chopped and used in pastries and desserts.

Serves 8 to 10

2 citrons, well washed

4 clementines, well washed

2¹/4 pounds superfine sugar

4 cups water

9 ounces good-quality dark chocolate (minimum 64% cocoa solids)

Cut the citrons in half straight through the center. Scrape out and discard the small central area of flesh. Now slice each half into 5 slices. Do this with the second fruit—giving you 20 slices altogether. Slice the clementines into circles, leaving on the skin.

Place all the fruit in a large pan and cover with cold water. Bring to a boil over low heat and simmer for 10 minutes, then drain. Repeat this process twice more—so that the fruit has been blanched and drained 3 times.

Return the fruit to the pan and add the sugar and 4 cups water. Stir carefully over low heat until the sugar has dissolved. Continue to cook the fruit very gently until it becomes translucent, about 30 minutes. Turn off the heat and let the fruit cool slowly in the sugar syrup for 30 minutes or so.

Drain the fruit and arrange the pieces on a wire rack over a tray (as shown on the previous page) or on a sheet of nonstick parchment paper, making sure that they are not touching each other. Let dry, uncovered, overnight.

The next day, break up the chocolate into a heatproof bowl and set over a pan of gently simmering water (making sure the water is not in contact with the bowl). Let melt gently, without stirring. Remove the bowl from the heat. Dip the candied clementine wheels into the chocolate one by one to half-coat them, then lay on waxed paper to dry. Do the same with the citron slices. Once set, store in an airtight container and refrigerate. Use within a few days.

Citrons, or *cedros* as they are known in Italy, look like large knobbly lemons. They have very little actual flesh, but are prized for their pith. This is thick, creamy, and much less bitter than the pith of lemons or oranges— making it perfect to candy.

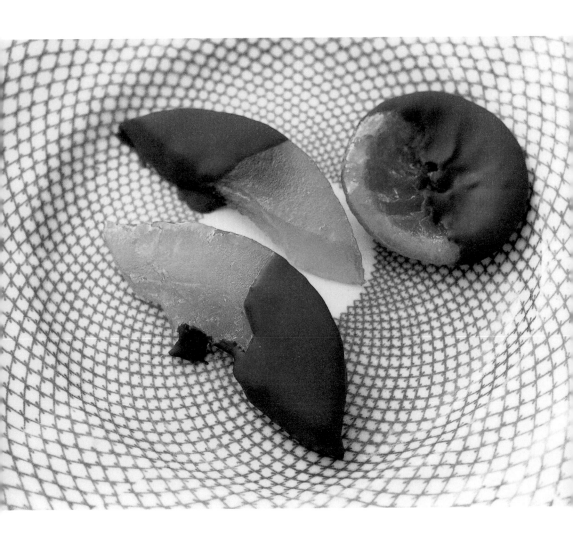

Beans & grains

Beans and grains are probably the mainstays of my cooking, appearing in different guises on the restaurant menu, but also in my cooking at home. They are primarily the foods that my children have grown up on—and what I crave to eat myself. Inexpensive and nutritious, it is no wonder that they feature so prominently in peasant cooking. They also transcend the seasons, as you can enjoy fresh beans during the summer months and the more familiar dried beans from fall through winter and spring.

Cooked with sympathetic flavorings, beans and grains not only taste delicious, but also are good for you. This is my favorite kind of food—when I eat, I like to feel that my body is benefiting from what I am putting into it. That is not to say that I am preoccupied with health in any way—health fads are strange to me and dull food is inexcusable to my mind. I want to eat food that is satisfying and full of flavor, and this is what I endeavor to cook.

We grow cranberry beans in our vegetable garden. They climb on willow cages skillfully constructed by Lucy, our gardener, every couple of years. Magenta and cream in color, these beans are one of nature's wonders as their colors are reversed inside the pods. Strangely, once cooked, they turn a mousy brown, but what they lose in beauty they make up for in flavor.

Among my favorite beans and grains are beautiful cranberry beans, cannellini beans, little lentils from Puy or Umbria, arrocina—a lovely little white bean from Spain—farro from Italy, and coco beans, which I've only ever encountered fresh during the summer. During the summer months, we shell fresh beans and cook them briefly until tender. In winter, we soak dried beans overnight and braise them slowly and gently to serve with slow-cooked lamb or beef, or to add in moderation to seafood stews. It is important not to overdo it, though, or you'll make the dish feel heavy.

◊

Dried beans are available all year round, but ideally you want to be cooking last year's harvest. Buy from specialty stores, such as Middle Eastern or Italian or Greek, where you think the turnover is likely to be high and therefore the produce fresh.

Ideally, dried beans should always be soaked overnight, then drained and cooked with herbs, garlic, perhaps a tomato or two, and a dried chile. Never add salt until they begin to soften, as it toughens the skins. If, like me, remembering to presoak beans is beyond your usual level of organization, there is a way round. Rinse the beans, place them in a pan, and cover with cold water, then bring to a boil. Drain, return to the pan, and cover a second time with cold water flavored with aromatics or whatever the recipe demands, then cook as if the beans have been presoaked.

◊

One of the things I love about beans and grains more than anything else is their ability to absorb flavors. This is most apparent if you dress them while hot with extra virgin olive oil, a good-quality red wine vinegar, or lemon juice, sea salt, Parmesan, and herbs—sage or rosemary in the winter; basil, mint, or parsley during spring and summer; marjoram, thyme, or oregano in the fall. Other flavorings that go with all beans and grains are garlic, fresh and dried chile, ripe tomatoes, duck, red meat, fish and shellfish, cream, and smoky bacon.

Farro (shown left), in particular, has an amazing ability to absorb flavors. I've fallen in love with this grain in recent years, eating it at every opportunity. One of the most ancient of all grains, it is said to have given the Roman foot soldiers the strength to conquer Europe. Known also as emmer wheat, it is no longer fashionable except in Italy, where it is used in soups, but I strongly urge you to try some.

Cranberry beans with garlic, sage, and olive oil

We make this dish in the summer with fresh cranberry beans from our garden. Without a doubt, these are my favorite fresh beans. Their beauty is mesmerizing, and their flavor rich and velvety. I eat them as often at room temperature as hot—tossed in a simple salad or with warm pasta. Even on toast, they are delicious.

Serves 6

2¹/4 pounds fresh cranberry beans, shelled

1 garlic bulb, split horizontally

bunch of sage

¹/4 cup red wine vinegar

generous 3/4 cup extra virgin olive oil

5 good-quality anchovy fillets, packed in salt or olive oil, rinsed if salted

Preheat the oven to 400°F (convection oven to 400°F). Put the beans into a baking dish, pour over enough water to cover them comfortably, then add all the rest of the ingredients. Cover the dish tightly with foil and place on the middle shelf of the oven. Cook until the beans are tender to the bite, 45 minutes to 1 hour.

Remove from the oven, stir well to combine, and let cool to room temperature. The beans should be full of the flavors with which they have been cooked and allowing them to stand will enhance this further.

Eat at room temperature or reheat the beans before serving—either by themselves or as an accompaniment to slow-cooked meats or broiled fish.

In winter when fresh cranberry beans are not available, I make this dish with good-quality dried beans, appreciating it even more on chilly days. Use half the quantity of beans. Soak overnight, then drain and proceed as above, allowing an extra half hour or so of cooking.

Chickpea and chard soup

More a meal than a soup, this is all I need to eat to pep me up at lunchtime during the week. Finished with a good splash of grassy, peppery, extra virgin olive oil, it is unctuous and truly lovely.

Serves 4

scant 1¹/4 cups dried chickpeas, soaked overnight

3 tbsp extra virgin olive oil, plus extra to serve

juice of ¹/2 lemon

2 dried red chiles

5 cloves garlic, peeled and smashed with the back of a knife

3 rosemary sprigs

2 (12-ounce) cans good-quality peeled plum tomatoes

sea salt and freshly ground black pepper

4 cups good-quality chicken stock (or water if you prefer)

10 ounces Swiss chard

2 slices of day-old, chewy, peasant-style bread, crusts removed

3 to 33/4 ounces Parmesan, freshly grated

Drain the chickpeas, rinse, and place in a large heavy pan. Cover generously with cold water, but do not season. Bring to a boil over medium heat, then turn down the heat. Simmer gently for 1¹/2 hours, or until the chickpeas are soft, skimming away any scum from the surface every now and then. Drain and dress with 1 tbsp of the olive oil and the lemon juice.

In the meantime, warm 2 tbsp of the olive oil in a separate pan over medium heat. Crumble in the chiles and add the garlic and rosemary. Cook for a minute or so to release the flavors, then add the tomatoes and stir well to break them up, adding a good pinch of salt. Cover and cook for 20 minutes, then pour in the stock and cook for another 10 minutes. Finally, add the cooked chickpeas and simmer gently for 40 minutes. Remove the rosemary sprigs.

Toward the end of the cooking time, prepare the chard. Wash and pat dry, then strip the leaves from the pale central stalk, using a small sharp knife; set aside. Trim the stalks and cut into ¹/2-inch chunks. Add these to a pan of well-salted boiling water and cook for 2 minutes, then add the soft green outer leaves and cook for another minute. Drain.

Break the bread into small pieces and stir into the soup along with 3 ounces of the Parmesan, turning the heat to low. Add the chard and a drizzle of olive oil. Taste and adjust the seasoning. The soup should be deeply flavorful and thick. Add a little more Parmesan and/or olive oil if needed. Ladle into warm soup plates and serve.

Chickpeas are harvested and dried at the end of the summer. Try to buy dried beans from the new season's harvest, as these will be the sweetest and most tender of all.

Cranberry beans, clams, and fino

The combination of fresh clams and fino sherry is a marriage made in heaven. Cranberry beans are equally at home here, as they mop up all the lovely flavors and pad out the dish. Salty, deep, and delicious, this dish is one I never tire of.

Serves 4

3 pounds fresh clams

1 fennel bulb, trimmed and tough outer layer removed

4 to 5 tbsp extra virgin olive oil

1 dried red chile

3 cloves garlic, peeled and crushed

9 ounces peeled plum tomatoes (from a can)

sea salt and freshly ground black pepper

generous 3/4 cup fino sherry

2 1/4 cups cooked cranberry beans

bunch of Italian parsley, leaves stripped and roughly chopped

Pick over the clams, discarding any that are damaged or open and do not close when gently squeezed. To clean the clams, simply leave them immersed in cold water for 20 minutes or so.

Roughly chop the fennel. Heat 2 tbsp of the olive oil in a heavy pan (large enough to hold all the ingredients comfortably) over medium heat. Add the fennel and cook gently for 5 minutes.

Crumble in the chile, and add the garlic and tomatoes. Stir well to combine and break up the tomatoes. Season with a small pinch of salt, bearing in mind the saltiness of the clams. Let bubble gently for about 10 minutes to reduce the tomatoes slightly and bring out the warmth of the chile and flavor of the garlic.

Add the clams and sherry. Cover the pan with a tight-fitting lid, turn up the heat to high, and cook for about 3 minutes. Once the clams have opened, add the cranberry beans and warm through.

Drizzle in the rest of the olive oil and sprinkle over the parsley. Stir well to combine and add a good grinding of pepper. Taste and adjust the seasoning if necessary— the flavor should be salty and unctuous with a marked dryness, which is the fino's contribution. Ladle into warm soup plates and serve immediately.

Clams like to feel they are still in the sea, so store them in the refrigerator in a covered bowl of cold water with a pinch of salt added until you are ready to cook them.

Wild garlic and white bean curry

The beauty and subtlety of wild garlic makes this dish very appealing, and fresh curry leaves add a fragrance that is quite seductive. During the summer months, we shell fresh coco beans and cook them directly in the curry until soft. In winter, we soak dried cannellini beans overnight and precook them in water for an hour or so over gentle heat, with one or two herbs added for flavor. I like to serve this curry just as it is, but you could add chunks of white fish to it.

Serves 6

1 tsp vegetable oil

2 red onions, peeled and finely sliced

1¹/2 tsp coriander seeds

1 tsp yellow mustard seeds

1 tsp fenugreek seeds

seeds from 5 cardamom pods

3 fresh red chiles (or more if you like heat), sliced (seeded if you prefer less heat)

12 fresh curry leaves

6 kaffir lime leaves

small handful of cilantro stems, washed and minced

4 cloves garlic, peeled and crushed

2 tbsp jaggery or superfine sugar

juice of 2 limes

3 tbsp fish sauce

2 (12-ounce) cans good-quality peeled plum tomatoes

2 cups shelled fresh coco beans, or 1 cup dried cannellini beans, cooked (see above)

generous 3/4 cup coconut milk

10 ounces wild garlic leaves

Heat the oil in a large heavy pan over medium-low heat and sweat the onions until soft and translucent.

In a separate pan, warm all the spice seeds until they release their fragrance and just begin to jump in the pan. Tip into a mortar and grind with the pestle while still warm.

Add the warm ground spices to the onions along with the chiles, curry leaves, lime leaves, and cilantro. Cook for another 5 minutes over fairly low heat, then add the garlic, jaggery, lime juice, and fish sauce. Stir well and cook for 5 minutes.

Add the tomatoes, stir well, and cook for another 10 minutes, then add the fresh or cooked dried beans and coconut milk. Cook gently for 10 to 15 minutes (or until the beans are tender if cooking fresh).

While the curry is cooking, wash the wild garlic very well, picking over each leaf thoroughly for they can carry little stones.

A couple of minutes before serving the curry, add the wild garlic and cook until it is just wilted and soft. Don't overcook it—wild garlic should be bright and vibrant. Taste and adjust the seasoning if necessary. This curry should be soft, fragrant, gently sweet, sharp, and salty, with just enough heat to warm you.

Broiled rabbit with lentils cooked in red wine

I love rabbit, specifically farmed rabbit, which has a gentle, clean flavor—less gamey than wild rabbit—and doesn't come riddled with shot. Here I've broiled the legs, which respond well to quick cooking, and served them on a bed of earthy lentils cooked in red wine with lots of flavorings. These full-bodied lentils are equally good with simply roasted chicken or broiled wild salmon, or tossed warm in a lightly dressed arugula and goat cheese salad. (Shown on previous page.)

Serves 4

4 farmed rabbit legs (ask your butcher for meaty back legs)

sea salt and freshly ground black pepper

olive oil, to brush

Lentils in red wine

1 cup small Umbrian or Puy lentils

3 tbsp olive oil

1 yellow onion, peeled and chopped

3 celery stalks, trimmed and chopped

3 carrots, peeled and chopped

4 slices of pancetta

small bunch of lemon thyme (or ordinary thyme)

3 bay leaves

2 cloves garlic, peeled and chopped

scant 2 cups full-bodied red wine, such as Barolo or Barbaresco

sea salt and freshly ground black pepper

2 tsp butter

1 tbsp minced parsley

Mustard and crème fraîche dressing

1/2 tbsp Dijon mustard

1 tsp sherry vinegar

generous 3/4 cup crème fraîche

sea salt and freshly ground black pepper

First cook the lentils. Wash them well, drain, and set aside. Heat the olive oil in a heavy pan, then add the onion, celery, carrots, and pancetta. Cook gently over low heat for 15 minutes, or until the vegetables are soft and sweet. Add the lentils, thyme, bay leaves, and garlic and stir well to combine.

Now pour in a third of the wine and turn up the heat slightly. Stir until the lentils have absorbed the wine, before adding another third (rather like making a risotto, but the wine is not added hot). When the second lot of wine is absorbed, add the rest. The lentils may still be a little hard once all the wine has been absorbed, in which case you'll need to add some water.

Continue cooking until the lentils are just tender to the bite—this may take as long as 40 minutes. Season well with salt and pepper and finish with the butter and minced parsley. (You can prepare these lentils a few hours in advance.)

For the dressing, combine the mustard and vinegar in a bowl, then whisk in the crème fraîche until smooth. Season with salt and pepper to taste.

When ready to serve, preheat the broiler to high. Season the rabbit legs generously all over with salt and pepper and brush with olive oil. Lay them on the broiler rack and broil on one side for 4 minutes, then turn and cook for 4 minutes on the other side. Check that the rabbit is cooked through.

To serve, spoon the lentils onto warm plates and lay a rabbit leg on each plate. Spoon over the mustard and crème fraîche dressing and serve at once.

Farinata

Farinata is a specialty of Genoa. A simple thick crêpe made of chickpea flour, it is traditionally baked in a wood-fired oven and served on its own or with Dolcelatte. I love it so much that I've even dreamt at night about eating it! Poor man's food—eaten by fishermen early in the morning before leaving on the day boats from Genoa harbor—it is hearty and sustaining.

Serves 6

scant 1¾ cups chickpea flour

sea salt and freshly ground black pepper

¼ cup extra virgin olive oil, preferably Ligurian, plus extra to serve

few rosemary sprigs, leaves only, chopped (optional)

1 cup sparkling water

1 tbsp olive oil

Dolcelatte, to serve (optional)

Put the flour into a bowl with 1 tsp salt and a little pepper and make a well. Pour in the extra virgin olive oil and add the rosemary, then whisk in the sparkling water. Mix until you have a smooth batter, then set aside to rest for 20 minutes.

Preheat the oven to 425°F (convection oven to 400°F). Place a large nonstick ovenproof skillet over medium heat. When hot, add the 1 tbsp olive oil and swirl the skillet to ensure that the bottom is evenly coated. Gently ladle in the batter, turn down the heat slightly, and cook for 1 to 2 minutes.

Now transfer the skillet to the middle shelf of the oven and bake, without turning, until the crêpe is cooked through and golden brown, 10 to 15 minutes.

Slide the hot farinata onto a plate and cut into rough triangles. Top with the Dolcelatte and drizzle with a little olive oil. Sprinkle salt and pepper over the farinata and serve warm.

Chickpea flour is available from most good delicatessens and Middle Eastern food stores. Seek out a good-quality brand.

Tomatoes

There is something undeniably wonderful about the sharp, green smell of a tomato plant come midsummer. Put your nose up close to the vine and breathe in. The smell is quite unique—grassy, slightly peppery, pungent, and completely summery. In a way, it is a strange smell but I love it. For me, tomatoes are one of the great joys of a summer menu—whether they are properly ripe, soft, sweet, and fruity, or still green with a sharp flavor and tight, crunchy flesh. They come in all shapes and sizes— small and round, oval or teardrop, or the shape and size of an ox heart. And in a myriad of hues, from almost chocolate brown—through orange and yellow, striped and green—to perfectly ripe and gloriously red. Heirloom tomatoes, San Marzano, cherry, datterini, tiger, and cuore di bue are some of my favorite varieties.

Although it is possible to buy tomatoes all year round, I encourage you to respect their season—midsummer to early fall is when they are truly at their best. Silky, fragrant, and plump at this time of year, their flavor more than makes up for the months they are not in season. Tomatoes that grace supermarket shelves all year round tend to be of the dependable growing varieties. Sadly they rarely have more than a hint of flavor; bland and watery, they add little to any dish.

Instead, look in season for tomatoes that feel heavy for their size and just yield to the touch. Avoid buying fruit that is too soft. The color—whatever it may be—should be even and free of bruises and blemishes. Always keep tomatoes out of the refrigerator, as the cold arrests their perfume and flavor, and prevents them from reaching their full potential. Tomatoes that have overripened or begun to soften need not be wasted, however, as they can easily be made into a delicious tomato sauce for pasta (see opposite).

◊

Tomatoes have a natural affinity with nearly all herbs. The classic marriage of perfectly ripe tomatoes and basil is difficult to beat, but in early fall try tomatoes with the earthy flavor of sage; marjoram, rosemary, and oregano also work beautifully. Seasoning is very important. The crystal crunch of good-quality sea salt is the perfect foil for sweet tomato flesh—provided you use just the right amount. Olive oil—extra virgin—enhances the flavor, too. Really sweet tomatoes can take the more peppery olive oils. And a drizzle of good-quality red wine vinegar or viscous, mellow traditional balsamic is the perfect foil for their sweetness.

Cheese, as I am sure you know, has a happy partnership with tomatoes. Sharp young goat cheese, crumbly sheep's milk cheese, and the freshest, softest, gentlest buffalo mozzarella all work perfectly. Olives, capers, and anchovies love tomatoes, too. Finally, please don't forget their affinity with seafood—crab and lobster, in particular. Try the recipe on page 132... it is one of my favorites.

When perfectly ripe and sweet, tomatoes can be eaten in the manner of the fruit they are—just like an apple or pear—but perhaps with a pinch of sea salt. At their best, they need nothing else.

Slow-roasted tomatoes

These tomatoes have a delicious sweet, intense flavor. I add them to all kinds of dishes, including salads, vegetables, fish, red meat, and cheeses. They will keep in sterilized jars in the refrigerator for up to a month, but should be used within a week once opened.

Makes 1 medium jar

6 to 8 ripe plum tomatoes

2 tsp superfine sugar

2 tsp sea salt

2 tsp freshly ground black pepper

Preheat the oven to its lowest setting—probably 250°F. Halve the tomatoes lengthwise and lay them, cut side up, in a single layer on a large baking sheet. Mix together the sugar, salt, and pepper, then sprinkle over the cut surface of the tomatoes. Roast in the oven, undisturbed, for 3 to 4 hours until they shrivel up. Remove and let cool.

Refrigerate and use within a few days, or pack in sterilized jars, cover with extra virgin olive oil, seal, and store in the refrigerator.

Tomato sauce for pasta

There is nothing fancy about this sauce. It's just incredibly useful—and a good way to use less than perfect tomatoes. It keeps well in the refrigerator for 3 to 4 days. Alternatively, you can store it in sealed sterilized jars in the refrigerator for a month or two, but use within a few days once opened.

Makes about 4 cups

3 pounds very ripe tomatoes

1/2 cup extra virgin olive oil

1 large red onion, peeled and minced

3 cloves garlic, peeled and crushed

sea salt and freshly ground black pepper

3 bay leaves

4 to 5 thyme sprigs

1 dried red chile

Chop the tomatoes roughly, cutting away any blemishes and the stem. Remove the seeds, if you prefer. Warm the olive oil in a large heavy pan over low heat, add the onion, and sweat gently for 10 minutes until soft, stirring occasionally. Add the garlic, a good pinch of salt, the bay leaves, and thyme. Crumble in the dried chile and cook for another 5 minutes.

Add the tomatoes, stir well, and turn up the heat. Cook fairly rapidly for 20 minutes, stirring frequently to ensure the sauce doesn't catch on the bottom of the pan and burn. To achieve a rich, vibrant sauce, you need to cook it over high heat to evaporate the liquid; if it is too watery, it will taste bland. Taste and season with a little more salt if necessary and a few grindings of black pepper. Remove the bay leaves and thyme. Toss the sauce with cooked pasta to serve.

Sauce vierge

This is a classic French tomato vinaigrette, comprising ripe tomatoes, good olive oil, tarragon, basil, and one of my very favorite herbs—chervil. The beauty of this sauce lies in its fresh clean flavor and it really needs to be put together shortly before serving. It goes beautifully with simply broiled fish of any variety, especially salmon and very fresh, deliciously oily sardines. It is also very good with broiled beef or lamb.

Makes about 3 cups

2¼ pounds ripe, firm tomatoes, without bruises or blemishes

sea salt and freshly ground black pepper

bunch of chervil, leaves only

bunch of tarragon, leaves only

small bunch of basil, leaves only

1 tbsp good-quality red wine vinegar

½ cup extra virgin olive oil

Put a large pot of water on to boil. Using a little knife, mark a shallow cross in each tomato skin—don't cut too deeply, it should really only be a nick. Plunge the tomatoes into the boiling water and remove them almost immediately (after about 15 seconds) using a slotted spoon. The skin at the cross incision should have curled back. Once they are cool enough to handle, peel off the skin—it should come away very easily. Halve the tomatoes, scoop out and discard the seeds, then cut into small, neat slices or dice.

Put the tomatoes into a bowl and season well with salt and pepper. Mince the herbs and add them to the tomatoes. Drizzle over the vinegar, stir to combine, then pour over the olive oil. Use the sauce within an hour or two.

Tomato and bread soup

We make this soup in the early fall when there tends to be a glut of tomatoes in the vegetable garden and we are anxious not to waste any. Inevitably, some are in less than perfect condition—softening around the edges perhaps or with the odd bruise or blemish. These are best showcased in this lovely, nurturing, elegantly flavored soup. Based on the Tuscan *pappa al pomodoro*, it is a firm favorite of mine. This one is laced with garlic and sage, with just a hint of chile, but you could replace the sage with basil for a more traditional flavor if you prefer.

Serves 4 to 6

2¼ pounds ripe tomatoes

scant ⅓ cup good-quality extra virgin olive oil, plus extra to drizzle

3 cloves garlic, peeled and sliced into fine slivers

1 dried red chile

5 sage sprigs (purple or common)

sea salt and freshly ground black pepper

3 slices of day-old, chewy peasant-style bread

aged balsamic vinegar, to finish (optional)

Chop the tomatoes roughly, but don't bother to remove the seeds. Place a heavy pan over medium heat and add the olive oil. When the oil is warm but not hot, add the tomatoes, garlic, chile, and sage. Season with a good pinch of sea salt and a couple of grindings of black pepper. Turn down the heat to really low and cook for 40 minutes, stirring every now and then.

Tear the bread into rough chunks with your fingers and add to the soup. Don't stir though, just let the bread disintegrate into the soup; it will readily absorb the wonderful, deep, satisfying flavor of the cooked tomatoes. Discard the chile.

Ladle into soup plates and drizzle with a little more olive oil and the balsamic vinegar. This soup is best served warm, rather than hot.

Nectarine and tomato salad with prosciutto and buffalo mozzarella

Nectarine with tomato may seem an odd combination for a salad, but it is actually quite exquisite. As with all simple things, it relies heavily on the use of very good ingredients. The nectarines should be sweet and properly ripe, the tomatoes the same. Texturally it is a lovely salad—soft and very refreshing on a hot summer's day. It should be served just on the cool side of room temperature.

Serves 4

4 perfectly ripe nectarines

20 perfectly ripe little tomatoes, such as cherry tomatoes

lemon juice

4 tsp or so of good-quality extra virgin olive oil

sea salt and freshly ground black pepper

4 balls of buffalo mozzarella

12 basil leaves (ideally purple basil), shredded

8 fine slices of prosciutto

2 tbsp basil oil (see below)

aged balsamic vinegar, to drizzle (optional)

Cut the nectarines in half along their natural division, remove the pits, then cut each half into thin wedges. Halve the tomatoes. Place the nectarines and tomatoes in a bowl and sprinkle with a few drops of lemon juice. Drizzle over the olive oil and season with a little salt and pepper.

Tear the mozzarella balls in half with your fingers and lay 2 halves on each plate. Now build your salad, alternating the nectarine slices and tomatoes with basil and prosciutto, spooning a little basil oil between the layers and seasoning delicately as you go. Finish with a restrained drizzle of balsamic vinegar.

Serve at once, preferably with some really good chewy peasant-style bread drizzled with olive oil.

Basil oil is a vibrant, sludgy sauce that I use to finish many dishes. To make it, whiz the leaves from 3 large bunches of basil in a food processor with 1 peeled garlic clove and a good pinch each of salt and pepper until the basil is minced. With the motor running, slowly trickle in 3/4 cup extra virgin olive oil and blend until you have a green purée. Let stand for a few minutes, then taste and adjust the seasoning. Store in a jar in the refrigerator—it will keep for up to a week.

Squash and tomato curry with lime and coconut

This curry is full of big, bold, clean, clear flavors. I love the strength of its color—it looks warm and inviting, happy and confident on the plate. It is good eaten with any type of flat bread and a tangle of blanched chard or spinach leaves dressed with a squeeze of lime juice and a drop or two of olive oil. Kabocha is a winter squash with a sweet flavor and dense texture. Don't bother to peel off the skin—it is tender enough to eat.

Serves 4

1 medium kabocha or butternut squash

1 tbsp vegetable oil

1 red onion, peeled and finely sliced

3 cloves garlic, peeled and minced

1 fresh green chile, chopped (seeds left in)

10 curry leaves

1 tsp mustard seeds

1 tsp fennel seeds

2 tbsp superfine sugar, or to taste

2 tbsp fish sauce, or to taste

juice of 2 limes, or to taste

15 to 20 ripe little tomatoes

1 (12-ounce) can good-quality peeled plum tomatoes

generous 1 cup coconut milk

Using a large, very sharp knife, slice through the middle of the squash. Scoop out the seeds using a spoon, then slice into 2-inch wedges and set aside.

Place a heavy pan over medium heat. Add the oil and, when it is warm, add the onion. Lower the heat and cook for 10 minutes until the onion is soft and translucent. Add the garlic, chile, and curry leaves, and continue to cook gently.

Meanwhile, warm a small, nonstick skillet over medium heat, add the mustard and fennel seeds, and cook until they just begin to pop. Remove from the heat and pound to a powder, using a mortar and pestle. Add to the onion curry base, stir to combine, and cook gently for another 5 minutes.

Add the squash, stir again, and cook for 10 minutes, then add the sugar, fish sauce, and lime juice. It is really important to get the balance of flavors right at this stage, so now is the time to taste and assess. The curry should be pleasantly (not aggressively) hot, sweet (but not sickly), sour (but not so much that it makes you squint), and salty enough to underpin and ground the dish.

Once you feel the flavors are just right, add the ripe tomatoes, squishing them slightly between your fingers as you do so to help them release their lovely flavor. Add the plum tomatoes, too. Cook for another 20 to 25 minutes until the squash is tender when pierced with a fork. Pour in the coconut milk and cook for a final 5 minutes or so.

The tomato and coconut milk enrich the curry, giving it a depth and smoothness that complete the dish. Turn off the heat and let cool. Reheat the curry gently and thoroughly when you are ready to serve. Like many wet dishes, this one improves in flavor if allowed to cool and sit before reheating.

Lobster with white beans, tarragon, and tomatoes

I find the sweet, rich flesh of lobsters a real treat. We cook this dish primarily during the early months of summer, when small native lobsters are particularly good. Perfectly ripe cooked tomatoes and tarragon, with its faintly anise flavor, make it really special.

Serves 4

4 small live lobsters, about 1 pound 2 ounces each

1 3/4 cups shelled fresh white cannellini beans, or good-quality dried ones, soaked overnight

3 tbsp extra virgin olive oil

1 clove garlic, peeled and crushed

bunch of tarragon, leaves only

1 tbsp red wine vinegar

20 perfectly ripe little tomatoes, such as cherry tomatoes

sea salt and freshly ground black pepper

generous 1/3 cup Pernod

2 tsp butter

Put the lobsters in the freezer for an hour or two, to render them soporific. Then, to parcook them, place the lobsters in a pan and pour in enough cold water to cover them by about 6 inches. Turn up the heat as high as it will go and cook until the water is on the point of boiling. Turn off the heat and let the lobsters sit in the hot water for 1 minute. Using tongs, remove them and let cool.

Have a bowl on hand so you can save the delicious juices as you prepare the lobsters. Lay one on its back and slice down the middle from top to tail with a sharp knife. Remove the meat from the body and set aside on a plate. Twist off the small legs, cutting off and discarding the bits of feathery gill sticking to the knuckle ends. Lay the legs alongside the body. Twist off the claws, then using a pair of scissors, cut down the length of the arms and pull out the meat. Crack the claws with a mallet and gently remove the shell—to keep the flesh in one piece. Set aside with the rest of the meat. Repeat with the other lobsters. Now you can start cooking.

Preheat the oven to 375°F (convection oven to 350°F). Tip the beans into a baking dish, pour in the olive oil, and add water to cover generously. Stir in the garlic, half of the tarragon, and the vinegar. Now add the tomatoes, piercing each one with a sharp knife as you do so, to let their sweet juice ooze out during cooking. Season with salt, cover, and place in the oven. Cook until the beans are creamy and tender, 25 to 40 minutes for fresh beans; 1 to 1 1/4 hours for dried ones. Check the liquid from time to time, adding a little more water if needed. Once tender, set aside while you warm the lobster.

Pour the Pernod into a pan large enough to hold the lobster meat and warm over low heat. Add the lobster and reserved juices and warm through briefly, turning occasionally to ensure it is evenly heated. Remove with a slotted spoon and divide among warm bowls.

Turn up the heat to high and add the butter, whisking vigorously to combine. Add to the warm beans, stir in the remaining tarragon, and taste for seasoning. Ladle over the lobster and serve immediately. Broiled sourdough bread—rubbed with a whisper of garlic and brushed with the best quality olive oil—is perfect for mopping up the juices.

Sea bass with mint, tomatoes, and red onions

This is a lovely, simple way to serve filleted small fish. Use the sweetest possible onions and the ripest tomatoes. The addition of mint is surprising and delicious, giving the dish a fresh, clean taste. Get your fishmonger to clean and scale the fish for you, and to fillet it as well if you can.

Serves 4

4 sea bass fillets with skin, about 6½ ounces each

generous ⅓ cup extra virgin olive oil

3 sweet red onions, peeled and finely sliced

1 tsp fennel seeds

1 dried red chile

sea salt and freshly ground black pepper

handful of Italian parsley, leaves only, coarsely chopped

small bunch of mint, leaves only, coarsely chopped

4 ripe, sweet, juicy tomatoes, roughly chopped

1 tbsp sherry vinegar

1 tbsp olive oil, for cooking

Season the skin of fish generously and cook until it is crunchy. I urge you to eat the skin of all fish. When perfectly cooked, it adds an element to the final taste that completes the dish.

Set the sea bass fillets aside on a covered plate to allow them to come to room temperature.

Place a pan over low heat, pour in the extra virgin olive oil, and, when the oil is warm, add the onions. Cook very gently for about 30 minutes to bring out the gentle sweetness of the onions. Meanwhile, toast the fennel seeds in a dry skillet to release their flavor, then grind using a mortar and pestle.

Add the ground fennel seeds to the onions, crumble in the chile, and season with a little salt. Cook for another 10 minutes, still over very low heat. Add half of the parsley and mint, stir well, then add the tomatoes and vinegar. Turn up the heat a little and cook for 10 minutes. This sauce should taste very clean, so don't cook the tomatoes for too long.

Preheat the oven to 375°F (convection oven to 350°F). Season the fish well with salt and pepper, especially on the skin side. Place a nonstick ovenproof skillet over high heat. Pour in a little olive oil and when hot, lay the fish, skin side down, in the skillet. Cook for 2 to 3 minutes until the skin is golden brown. Immediately transfer the skillet to the oven to finish cooking without turning the fish. This should take no more than 2 to 3 minutes.

To serve, taste the sauce for seasoning and adjust if necessary, then add the rest of the parsley and mint. Spoon into warm shallow bowls and lay the fish fillets on top. Serve at once.

Rabbit with saffron, cucumber, tomatoes, and basil

I'm very partial to rabbit and it is always a popular choice when we have it on the menu, yet sadly it seems to be underrated in the UK. This combination, inspired by a dish in Richard Olney's *Simple French Food*, is exquisite. For hefty appetites, you might like to cook the smaller shoulders along with the legs—they have a lovely sweet flavor. We serve this dish with soft polenta laced with lemon zest, unsalted butter, black pepper, and Parmesan.

Serves 6

6 farmed rabbit legs (and shoulders, if you like)

sea salt and freshly ground black pepper

2 tbsp olive oil

40 saffron threads

3 cloves garlic, peeled and finely sliced

3 cups verjuice

20 ripe little tomatoes, such as cherry tomatoes

4 little cucumbers

bunch of basil, leaves only

1 tbsp unsalted butter

Season the rabbit with salt and pepper. Place a large, wide pan over medium heat and add the olive oil. When it is hot, brown the rabbit in batches if necessary; don't overcrowd the pan. You want to brown the portions quite gently, but really thoroughly until they are golden brown all over.

Add the saffron and garlic, then pour in the verjuice, scraping up all the delicious juices from the bottom of the pan. Let bubble to reduce down a bit, then turn down the heat to low. Using the tip of a sharp knife, pierce each tomato and add to the pan. Season with a little more salt and pepper, then cover and cook gently for 30 minutes until the rabbit is cooked through. Continue to cook slowly for another 15 minutes until the rabbit is very tender.

Meanwhile, halve the cucumbers lengthwise and scoop out the seeds, then halve each piece or cut into quarters. Add to the rabbit and cook for no more than a couple of minutes. Tear the basil into strips with your fingers and add to the pan along with the butter. Swirl to combine and immediately remove from the heat. Taste one last time and adjust the seasoning if you need to, then serve.

Verjuice is made from the juice of unripe grapes. It is slightly tart and adds a little acidity without overpowering the flavors in this dish. If you can't find verjuice, use apple juice instead for this recipe and add a squeeze of lemon juice.

Lamb with tomatoes and horseradish dressing

This recipe showcases *cuore di bue*, large tomatoes from Italy the size and shape of an ox heart, hence the name. I prefer to use these tomatoes still slightly green, when their flavor is pleasantly sharp and refreshing. Here I combine them with grilled lamb and my favorite chard. I love all greens but, to me, nothing is nicer than properly cooked tender rainbow or Swiss chard with a good glug of olive oil—it tastes as if it is so good for you!

Serves 6

1 pound 2 ounces rainbow chard, washed

1/4 cup extra virgin olive oil, plus extra to brush

sea salt and freshly ground black pepper

3/4- to 1 1/4-inch piece fresh horseradish, peeled

1/4 cup red wine vinegar

1 boned leg of lamb, about 3 pounds, trimmed of most of its fat and cut into 6 generous slices

2 cuore di bue tomatoes or other large meaty tomatoes, cut into slices 1/8 inch thick

Heat up your grill or broiler, as it needs to be really hot in order to give the lamb a lovely strong crust and flavor.

Bring a large pot of well-salted water to a boil. Plunge the chard into the boiling water and cook for 2 to 3 minutes, then drain in a colander (but don't refresh). Dress, while warm, with the 1/4 cup olive oil and season with a little salt and pepper. Set aside until you are ready to serve.

Grate the horseradish, place in a small bowl, and pour over the vinegar. Season with a little salt (but no pepper) and set aside.

Brush the lamb with olive oil and season generously with salt and pepper. Lay on the grill or under the broiler and cook for 3 minutes without moving, then turn the slices and cook on the other side for 3 minutes. Remove to a plate and set aside in a warm place to rest for 5 minutes or so.

To serve, cut the lamb into slices 1/2 inch thick. Lay a slice of tomato on each plate, arrange a little chard on top, then add a slice of lamb and spoon over a little horseradish dressing. Continue layering until the lamb, chard, and tomatoes are all used. This dish is best served at room temperature.

Eating food at room temperature is one of the best ways to experience subtle nuances of flavor. For me, it is the ideal way to experience many tastes—perhaps that's why I am so fond of salads.

Tomato and apple ketchup

At the beginning of fall, when the last of the summer tomatoes
are still around and the earliest apples are creeping in, it is time to
make ketchup. Good homemade tomato ketchup is a delight. Sweet
and zingy, it is the perfect accompaniment to beef or hamburgers,
sharp cheddars, and lemony goat cheeses—though you only need a
tiny amount with these delicately flavored soft cheeses.

Makes two 1-pound jars

1 tbsp olive oil

5 red onions, peeled and
roughly chopped

2¹/4 pounds apples

5¹/2 pounds ripe tomatoes

2 cloves garlic, peeled and
minced

2 cups superfine sugar

2 cups red wine vinegar

10 cloves

2 cinnamon sticks

3 bay leaves

12 juniper berries

sea salt and freshly ground
black pepper

Place a preserving kettle or a large heavy pan over low heat and add
the olive oil. When it is warm, tip in the onions and sweat gently for
10 minutes until soft and translucent. Meanwhile, core and roughly
chop (but do not peel) the apples and tomatoes.

Add the garlic to the pan and sweat for 1 minute, then add the apples
and tomatoes. Stir in the sugar and vinegar. Tie the spices, bay
leaves, and juniper berries in a piece of cheesecloth and drop into the
pan. Stir the mixture to combine all the ingredients, then turn down
the heat to low and cook for 1¹/2 hours, stirring occasionally to make
sure the mixture doesn't stick on the bottom of the pan.

The ketchup is ready when it has cooked right down to a glossy,
pulpy sauce. Discard the cheesecloth bundle. Add a generous pinch
of salt and a few grindings of pepper. Let cool, then spoon into two
1-pound sterilized jars. Seal and store in a cool, dark place. Use
within a few months and keep in the refrigerator once opened.

Made in generous quantities and stored in sterilized jars,
this ketchup will keep happily in the refrigerator or a cool, dark pantry
throughout the fall and even into the start of winter—providing a taste
of warmth to dishes in the cooler months.

Nuts

*Last fall, on a warm, sunny day, I had an unforgettable
simple lunch on a lavender farm just outside Melbourne.
The crop was being harvested and the heady scent of
lavender was everywhere. A table was laid under a huge,
old walnut tree and all around underfoot were young pale-
colored walnuts. Their shells broke effortlessly. Crisp to
the bite and very sweet, these beautiful nuts were a
memorable taste and a joyful reminder of the turning
of the season.*

    *Nuts provide both textural depth and flavor to dishes in
a way that nothing else is really quite able to. I love this
quality and use all sorts of nuts in my cooking, especially
during the fall and winter. Young, sweet hazelnuts and
cobnuts (a variety of hazelnuts) are among my favorites…
and creamy fresh walnuts, of course. As with all nuts,
freshness is of the utmost importance, so buy them in the
shell if you possibly can—and treat them with respect, as
they are delicate and easily spoilt.*

Sadly, nuts are often not at their peak when they arrive in the stores for us to buy. Although regarded as pantry ingredients, they are fragile and perishable, soon losing their freshness and turning rancid. So, wherever possible, nuts should be bought in their shell, in small quantities, and kept in a sealed container in a cool dark place. They really need to be eaten within a couple of weeks of purchase, at the most.

Walnuts are probably the most delicate of all nuts. Their flavor declines rapidly once they are removed from their shell, turning bitter and sharp. Sweet, creamy "wet walnuts" as they are known when young and freshly shelled, are altogether different and probably the best crop of the year.

◊

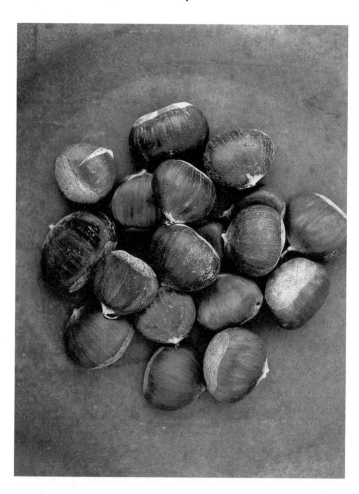

Different nut varieties work better with different ingredients. You may well have your own ideas and preferences, but here is my rough guide to pairing nuts with other foods:

Almonds work well with chocolate, honey, peaches, nectarines, and apricots. They are also lovely with delicate pink-fleshed fish like trout and salmon, but also with rabbit and succulent little birds such as pigeon or quail. In Spain, ground or minced almonds are often used to thicken dishes, providing texture as well as a creamy, sweet richness.

Cashews, candlenuts, and peanuts have a natural affinity with chile, tamarind, mint, cilantro, cucumber, lime, coconut milk, white fish, chicken, and white rice.

Chestnuts are lovely with meringues, confectioners' sugar, and cream. In savory dishes, they work well with prosciutto, sage, game birds, porcini, potatoes, Brussels sprouts, and winter greens.

Hazelnuts are beautiful with many cheeses, especially hard cow's milk cheeses, but also in a salad with warm game and pickled fruit. Pounded into a thick paste and laced with orange zest, they will enhance broiled pork, beef, and lamb. And, of course, hazelnuts are perfect with chocolate and honey.

Pecans go well with maple syrup, cream, bananas, and caramel, as well as blue cheeses, dates, beet, and avocados.

Pine nuts go with basil, Parmesan, romano, and olive oil to make pesto, obviously, but also with pasta, spinach, raisins, quail, and most salad leaves.

Walnuts are lovely with crisp sweet apples and pears, blue cheeses, game, watercress, and other bitter greens. And when creamy and fresh, they are sublime pounded into a paste with garlic, lemon zest, and parsley, or bread crumbs, roasted tomatoes, and dried chiles to serve with meat or white fish.

◊

Whenever you are serving nuts or using them in cooking, first warm or toast them gently in the oven to tickle out their flavor, if not to color them. The heat of the oven heightens their taste and fragrance and gives them a better bite. Lastly, when grinding nuts, do use a mortar and pestle to pound them. To my mind, a blender or food processor is too aggressive for nuts and spoils their flavor.

Nut oils feature strongly in my cooking during the fall. I love to drizzle walnut or hazelnut oil over broiled lamb or beef, and these oils are charming with leaves such as frisée and watercress.

Salad of roasted beets, walnuts, watercress, and mascarpone

I love the gentle sweetness of beets—they taste to me quite simply of the earth from which they have been pulled. My favorite way to cook them is roasted in their skins, while they are still young and small. Warm from the oven, they work so nicely with walnuts and watercress. This salad makes a good first course or you can serve it as part of a larger spread.

Serves 4

12 small beets

1 tbsp plus 2 tsp aged balsamic vinegar

2 tbsp olive oil

sea salt and freshly ground black pepper

generous handful of watercress, trimmed

20 creamy young "wet" walnuts in the shell

3/4 to scant 1 cup mascarpone

lemon juice

1/4 cup walnut oil

Preheat the oven to 375°F (convection oven to 350°F). Wash the beets well to remove any dirt, but leave their skins on. If they have little roots, leave them on as they create a lovely heap on the plate.

Place the beets in a roasting pan and drizzle over 1 tbsp of the vinegar and the olive oil. Season with salt and pepper and cover the pan tightly with the foil. Roast on the middle shelf of the oven for 30 to 35 minutes, then remove the foil and cook until the skins are wrinkly and the beets feel tender when pierced with a skewer, 10 to 15 minutes.

Meanwhile, wash the watercress and pat dry. Crack open the walnuts (I give them a gentle tap with a rolling pin) and extract the nuts. Arrange the watercress and warm beets on individual plates. Spoon the mascarpone on top and squeeze over the lemon juice, with a light touch.

Scatter the walnuts over the salad, then drizzle over the remaining 2 tsp vinegar and the walnut oil. Season with salt and pepper and serve, while the beets are still just warm.

The importance of texture in cooking cannot be underestimated. All things must be considered on tasting–flavor first and always, but also how the food feels in your mouth.

Roasted Jerusalem artichokes with goat cheese, roasted tomatoes, and agresto

Agresto is a soft, rounded, pounded paste made with very fresh, young, creamy walnuts. It works very well with the rich, nutty flavor of roasted Jerusalem artichokes and sweet, lightly roasted tomatoes. The goat cheese lends a gentle lemony acidity, which rounds the dish off.

Serves 4

12 Jerusalem artichokes (sunchokes)

1/4 cup olive oil

sea salt and freshly ground black pepper

12 little plum or cherry tomatoes

1/2 tbsp good-quality red wine vinegar

4 slices of chewy peasant-style bread

1 clove garlic, peeled

extra virgin olive oil, to drizzle

generous handful of salad leaves, such as arugula

7 ounces young, light goat cheese

Agresto

20 creamy young "wet" walnuts in the shell

2 good-quality salted anchovy fillets

1 clove garlic, peeled

1 dried red chile, minced

1 small bunch of Italian parsley, leaves only, chopped

finely grated zest and juice of 1 lemon

generous 3/4 cup extra virgin olive oil

sea salt and freshly ground black pepper

First make the agresto. Crack open the walnuts (I give them a gentle tap with a rolling pin) and extract the nuts. Place a handful of them in a large mortar and start to pound gently with the pestle, gradually adding the rest of the nuts. Add the anchovies and garlic and continue to pound—the sauce should be smooth and creamy in parts, roughly textured in others. Stir in the chile, parsley, lemon zest, and juice, then gradually incorporate the olive oil. Taste and adjust the seasoning—adding a little salt if necessary and a good grinding of pepper. Set aside while you roast the artichokes.

Preheat the oven to 425°F (convection oven to 400°F). Scrub the artichokes under cold running water to remove the dirt, but don't bother to peel them. Cut in half lengthwise and place in a roasting pan. Drizzle over 3 tbsp of the olive oil, season generously with salt and pepper, and toss to coat well. Roast on the middle shelf of the oven until the artichokes are golden brown and tender, 25 to 40 minutes.

Halfway through cooking the artichokes, place the tomatoes in a separate roasting pan, season with salt and pepper, and spoon over the vinegar and 1 tbsp of the olive oil. Roast on the top shelf of the oven until the tomatoes are soft and beginning to split from their skins, 10 to 15 minutes. Set aside in a warm place with the artichokes while you toast the bread.

Preheat the broiler and toast the slices of bread until golden brown on both sides. Once the bread is a really good color, remove from the broiler and rub gently on one side with the garlic. Drizzle with a little extra virgin olive oil and season with a pinch of sea salt.

Place a slice of bruschetta on each plate. Arrange the artichokes, salad leaves, and tomatoes on top and crumble over the goat cheese. Spoon on the agresto and serve at once, while still warm.

Squid with arugula and romesco

Romesco is one of the great nut-based sauces of Spain. We serve it in all sorts of ways—with grilled meats or game; with seafood such as sautéed shrimp with wilted spinach; even scattered over grilled spicy chorizo with a handful of lightly dressed arugula. Romesco can be based on almonds alone, but adding hazelnuts gives the sauce a more complex flavor. It is best used on the day it is made.

Serves 4

1 pound 2 ounces small squid, with tentacles

sea salt and freshly ground black pepper

3 tbsp olive oil

Salad

small handful of mint, leaves only

handful of basil, leaves only

handful of arugula leaves

juice of 1 lemon

1/4 cup extra virgin olive oil

sea salt and freshly ground black pepper

Romesco

1/3 cup shelled almonds

1/4 cup shelled hazelnuts

2 ripe tomatoes

1 large fresh red chile

4 cloves garlic, peeled

sea salt

1 tsp sweet paprika

1 tbsp red wine vinegar

4 tbsp fresh coarse white bread crumbs

generous 1/3 cup extra virgin olive oil

To serve

lemon wedges

To clean the squid, hold the body with one hand and pull out the head with the tentacles attached, using the other hand; most of the innards will come too. Peel off the skin at the same time. Cut the tentacles from the head, discarding the head, eyes, and hard beak. Remove the transparent quill from the body and the soft gooey matter. Rinse the body pouch and tentacles gently under cold running water, drain, and set aside in a cool place.

For the romesco, preheat the oven to 375°F (convection oven to 350°F). Place the nuts on a baking sheet and roast on the middle oven shelf until golden, 3 to 6 minutes. Tip the hot nuts into a clean dry cloth and rub to remove the skins. Place the tomatoes and chile on a baking sheet and roast for 6 to 10 minutes, turning halfway through cooking, until the tomatoes are slightly colored and bursting from their skins, and the chile is soft—it might take an extra minute or two.

Put the garlic and a pinch of salt into a large mortar and crush with the pestle to a rough paste, then add the chile and crush. Add the roasted nuts and pound until the paste is fairly smooth, but still retains some texture. Add the tomatoes and paprika and continue to pound, but more gently now. Stir in the vinegar, bread crumbs, and olive oil. Season to taste and set aside.

For the salad, wash the herb and salad leaves, pat dry, and place in a large bowl. Drizzle over the lemon juice and olive oil, season with salt and pepper, and toss lightly to combine.

Heat one large or two smaller nonstick skillets over fairly high heat. Season the squid well all over with salt and pepper and add a little olive oil to the skillet(s). Once the oil is hot, add the squid, being careful not to overcrowd the skillet. Cook undisturbed for 1 minute, then turn and cook for a minute on the other side.

Tip the squid into the bowl of dressed leaves and toss to combine the flavors. Arrange on warm plates and crumble over the romesco. Serve immediately with lemon wedges for squeezing.

Skirt steak is a less common cut of beef, but it has an excellent flavor and is well worth seeking out. A lean cut from the inner thigh with elongated fibers, it's best served rare, sliced against the grain.

Skirt steak with hazelnut picada and wilted escarole

Picada hails from Spain, or more specifically, from Catalonia. Flavored with nuts, bread crumbs, and herbs, it is a punchy, vibrant paste—often used as a sauce to enliven dishes and to thicken stews. Here it partners with full-flavored skirt steak and elegant escarole lettuce, which is just wilted to serve as a vegetable. Like romesco, there are plenty of other uses for picada, if you have any left over.

Serves 4

1¹/2 pounds skirt steak, cut into 4 portions

1 head of escarole

sea salt and freshly ground black pepper

extra virgin olive oil, to brush

4 tbsp unsalted butter

Picada

1 thick slice of chewy peasant-style bread

generous 3/4 cup extra virgin olive oil

20 shelled hazelnuts

grated or finely shredded zest of 1 orange

1 tbsp orange juice

1 clove garlic, peeled

small bunch of oregano, leaves only

sea salt

Set the steaks aside on a covered plate to bring them to room temperature.

For the picada, preheat the oven to 375°F (convection oven to 350°F). Tear the bread roughly into pieces. Heat the olive oil in a shallow pan over medium heat. When it is hot, add the bread and fry until evenly golden and crisp. (Take care that the olive oil does not become too hot and begin to smoke.) Remove and drain off excess oil. Pound the bread, in batches if necessary, using a mortar and pestle, until you have coarse bread crumbs.

Place the nuts on a baking sheet and roast in the middle of the oven until evenly golden, 5 to 10 minutes. Tip the hot nuts into a clean dry cloth and rub to remove the skins. Mince the nuts and place in a bowl with the bread crumbs, orange zest, and juice. Mince the garlic and oregano together and add to the bowl with a pinch of salt. Stir to combine, then set aside. Turn the oven to its lowest setting.

Discard the outer leaves from the escarole, then tear into large pieces. Wash well, but don't bother to pat dry.

Season the steaks liberally all over. Place a heavy skillet over high heat and brush the steaks with a little olive oil. Lay the steaks in the skillet when it is hot and cook without moving for 3 minutes. Turn and cook on the other side for 3 minutes (you may need a minute or two longer if the steaks have been cut from a thicker section of the thigh). You should have a nice brown crust, while the meat inside should be rare. Remove to a plate and let rest in the warm oven for 4 to 8 minutes.

Meanwhile, cook the escarole. Place a wide pan over medium-low heat. Add the butter and let it just melt, then add the torn leaves and salt and pepper. Put the lid on until the water clinging to the leaves begins to steam, then uncover and stir every few seconds so the leaves wilt uniformly. This will take 2 to 3 minutes. Now you should have a lovely glossy, pale green vegetable. Check the seasoning.

Place a steak on each warm serving plate and arrange the escarole alongside. Spoon over the picada and serve at once.

Warm date and almond puddings

These cozy, warm little desserts are just the sort of thing I like to eat when the weather turns cool. Like most people, I tend to have dessert as an occasional treat, rather than as a regular occurrence; these, however, I find almost impossible to resist. I like to eat them warm and steaming with thick cold cream—and sometimes a spoonful of warm honey, laced with grated lemon and orange zest.

Serves 6

1/2 cup plus 1 tbsp unsalted butter, plus extra to grease

all-purpose flour, to dust

3/8 cup light corn syrup, slightly warmed

12 Medjool dates

1 tbsp Pedro Ximénez sherry

2/3 cup superfine sugar

2 organic large eggs

scant 1/2 cup self-rising flour

small pinch of salt

1 tsp baking powder

1/3 cup ground almonds

finely grated zest of 1 orange

Butter and flour 6 individual ovenproof bowls, about 2/3 cup capacity. Set on a baking sheet and spoon 1 tbsp corn syrup into each of the molds (this will become the sticky topping). Set aside.

Remove the pits from the dates and chop them into small pieces. Place in a bowl and add the sherry and just enough boiling water to cover. Let soak for 10 minutes.

Preheat the oven to 375°F (convection oven to 375°F). Cream the butter and sugar together either by hand or using an electric mixer until soft, light, and creamy. Add the eggs, one at a time, beating well after each addition. (The mixture may appear to separate at this point, but it will come back together.)

Sift together the flour, salt, and baking powder, combine with the ground almonds, and fold into the batter with the orange zest. Squeeze out the excess moisture from the dates, add to the mixture, and stir well to combine.

Divide the batter among the ovenproof bowls, filling them no more than two-thirds full. Bake until well risen, golden, and springy to the touch, 20 to 25 minutes.

To unmold, run a small knife around the inside of each mold and invert the pudding onto a warm plate. Serve the little desserts at once, either on their own or, as I prefer, with a dollop of cream.

Hazelnut tart

This is a simple tart—both in flavor and in execution. These days I always make pie dough in the food processor—it is so much quicker and less messy than mixing it by hand. I prepare this tart most often in the fall, when the first nuts of the year begin to appear. My favorite way to serve it is with crème fraîche and sweet, tender fall raspberries.

Serves 8 to 10

Pie dough

13/4 cups all-purpose flour, sifted, plus extra to dust

1/2 cup plus 1 tbsp unsalted butter

2 tbsp superfine sugar

1 organic egg

1 organic egg yolk

grated zest of 1 lemon

1/2 tsp vanilla extract

Filling

2 cups hazelnuts

11/2 cups superfine sugar

3 organic eggs

finely grated zest of 1 lemon

11/4 cups unsalted butter, in pieces

For the dough, have all the ingredients well chilled. Tip the flour into a food processor. Cut the butter into tiny cubes, or grate it if you prefer. Add to the flour along with the sugar, whole egg, egg yolk, lemon zest, and vanilla. Now turn on the machine. The mixture will soon have a granular, moist texture, the consistency of wet sand. Keep going and it should soon gather into a ball. Just occasionally, you may find you need to add a little iced water to help it along—do this sparingly as it is easy to overdo it. Take out the dough, wrap it in plastic wrap, and let rest in the refrigerator for 30 minutes or so while you make the filling.

Preheat the oven to 375°F (convection oven to 375°F). Place the nuts on a baking sheet and roast on the middle shelf of the oven for 3 to 6 minutes—to tickle out their flavor and make the skins easier to remove. Rub the nuts in a clean dry cloth to remove the skins.

Place the nuts in a blender and add the sugar, eggs, lemon zest, and butter. Pulse to combine—keeping the nuts quite textural, rather than grinding them finely. Transfer to a bowl and set aside.

Lightly flour your counter and rolling pin and roll out the dough to a large circle, about 1/8 inch thick. Lift the dough onto the rolling pin and drape it over a 10-inch tart pan, about 1 inch deep, with removable bottom. Press the dough into the edges and sides of the pan and prick the base all over with a fork. Place in the refrigerator for 30 minutes to rest.

Line the pastry shell with waxed paper and dried beans and bake "blind" for 15 minutes. Remove the beans and paper and return the shell to the oven for another 5 minutes. Let cool slightly. Spoon in the hazelnut filling, distributing it evenly. Bake until golden and the filling is just soft in the center, 25 to 35 minutes. If it appears to be overbrowning, cover loosely with foil.

Let the tart cool to room temperature before slicing and serving, either on its own or with crème fraîche and raspberries.

Pecan and maple syrup ice cream

I make ice cream every day of the year, even through the winter months. Clean, gentle, and not too sweet, I find it is one of the nicest ways to finish a meal—light or heavy. No matter how bespoke some store-bought ice creams claim to be, I find homemade ice cream far superior. This is one of the sweeter ice creams we make, which is probably why it is always popular with children. Pecans and maple syrup have a natural affinity.

Serves 8

2 cups whole milk

1 vanilla bean, split lengthwise

10 organic egg yolks

$1/2$ cup superfine sugar

$1^1/2$ tbsp maple syrup, plus extra to drizzle

$1^1/4$ cups heavy cream

20 shelled pecans, plus a few extra to serve, roughly chopped

Pour the milk into a heavy pan. Scrape the seeds from the vanilla bean and add them to the milk, together with the empty bean. Place over low heat and slowly bring to just below a boil. Remove from the heat and let infuse for at least 30 minutes. Remove the vanilla bean.

Put the egg yolks and sugar in a bowl and whisk together thoroughly. Return the milk to medium-low heat. As soon as it comes to just under a boil, remove from the heat and add the maple syrup. Pour onto the egg yolk mixture, stirring with the whisk as you do so.

Pour the mixture back into the pan and stir over very low heat with a wooden spoon, using a figure eight motion, until the custard has thickened enough to lightly coat the back of the spoon. Don't overheat or it may curdle. As soon as it thickens, remove from the heat, pour into a bowl, and let cool completely.

Once cool, stir in the cream and churn in an ice-cream maker. When the ice cream begins to set, add the chopped pecans and continue to churn for another 10 minutes. Transfer the ice cream to a freezerproof container and place in the freezer for at least 2 hours before serving. It is best served within a day or two of making.

To serve, scoop the ice cream into bowls, sprinkle with a few chopped pecans, and add a drizzle of maple syrup.

An ice-cream maker is essential for smooth-textured ices and sorbets. You can now purchase relatively inexpensive machines for home use.

Vinegar

The sharp, clear, top note flavor of vinegar serves to hone and refine flavors in cooking. I use it as an enhancer in conjunction with other flavorings, to give a dish a sense of wholeness. In my cooking, vinegar is often married with the saltiness of anchovies, the warmth rather than heat of dried chiles, the lovely grassiness of olive oil, the fragrance of spices—such as fennel or coriander seeds—and base note herbs like sage and rosemary.

Vinegar, like olive oil or wine, has a host of different possibilities within its umbrella term—from thin and eye-squintingly sharp to rich, viscous, mellow, and even sweet. More often than not, I cook with the sharper vinegars—long, slow, gentle cooking softens the flavor, smoothing its edges. Of course, aged balsamic vinegar with its wonderfully complex, sweet flavor is in a class of its own. Just a few drops sprinkled onto a dish will impart a very special quality.

In my pantry I have several different varieties of vinegar, including cider, honey, white wine, and spiced vinegars, but the two I use most frequently are very good-quality red wine vinegar and sherry vinegar. I find sherry vinegar pairs beautifully with the first of the season's nut oils, especially hazelnut and walnut. In the fall, sherry vinegar comes into its own in my kitchen, as I use it to make vinaigrettes to dress seasonal salads comprising mushrooms, nuts, perhaps finely shaved fennel, some torn warm pheasant or pigeon, and maybe a few pickled fall grapes.

Red wine vinegar, on the other hand, I use more often in cooking. A splash invariably goes into slow-cooked pork and lamb dishes. And I like to add a drop or two when roasting tomatoes or cranberry beans or to flavor still-warm farro. On its own, the flavor can be too sharp, but paired with olive oil, herbs, and other flavorings—even Parmesan and butter—really beautiful and profound flavors can be achieved.

Malt vinegar is one variety I don't use in my cooking—its flavor is achingly sharp and thin, and it lacks the depth of traditionally made wine vinegars. I appreciated the harsh taste more as a child— sprinkled onto potato scallops (deep-fried, battered potato slices) from our local fish shop, which I loved at the time. So the flavor lingers in my memory, happily and evocatively!

◊

Balsamic vinegar is produced in a different way from the wine- or sherry-based vinegars described above. The base for balsamic vinegar is what the Italians call *cotto mosto*, which is essentially crushed grapes that are cooked in copper pots. No flavorings or additives are added. Aged naturally, the vinegar ferments in a series of wooden casks that range from cherry and juniper to oak and chestnut—in no particular order. Each wooden cask contributes its very own flavor to the final complex, dark amber vinegar. The taste is not sharp at all. It is best described as mellow, round, and sweet, with notes of honey, but still tasting very much of the grape from which it originated.

When buying balsamic vinegar, on the label look for the description *aceto balsamico tradizionale*—only this wording confirms the vinegar's authenticity. There are many poor imitations on the market that do not resemble the true product at all—sometimes no more than cheap vinegar flavored with caramel. True aged balsamic vinegar is unquestionably costly, but well worth the expense. You only need to use it sparingly—a drop or two is often enough to give a dish special character.

Good-quality vinegars can be expensive, but it really is worth using the best you can afford. Even when you are pickling fruit or making warm spicy chutneys or tomato ketchup, please don't skimp. The final taste of any dish can only be as good as the ingredients that have gone into its creation.

Bruschetta with aged balsamic vinegar

We occasionally serve this at the restaurant as something to nibble on with an aperitif. It is very simple, but delicious—a lovely way to showcase the beautiful rich depth of a *balsamico tradizionale*. I like to use a peasant-style bread without salt, such as pane toscano, pagnotta pugliese, or a good-quality ciabatta. I prefer to sprinkle the salt on myself once the bread is toasted, lightly rubbed with garlic, doused with olive oil, and finished off with just a trickle of balsamic vinegar.

Serves 4

4 slices of good-quality chewy, peasant-style bread, cut about 1/2 inch thick

1 clove garlic, peeled

2 tbsp good-quality mild-tasting extra virgin olive oil

4 tsp aged balsamic vinegar

sea salt

minced parsley, to finish (optional)

Preheat your broiler or grill and toast the slices of bread until golden on both sides. Remove from the broiler or grill and, while still warm, rub gently all over with the garlic clove. Cut the slices in half and brush with the olive oil.

Drizzle over the vinegar and sprinkle with salt and a little minced parsley. Serve at once, while still warm. Delicious with a glass of sparkling wine.

Pickled pumpkin with burrata

This pairing of sweet, sharp pickled pumpkin slices with Burrata—a gentle, creamy, rich, cow's milk mozzarella from Puglia in Italy—makes a delectable first course. You'll have more pickled pumpkin than you need here, but it is worth making a reasonable quantity because it is lovely with so many things. Try it with slow-cooked veal; or smoked eel topped with a dollop of crème fraîche, laced with grated horseradish; or chopped and tossed in a salad of lentils and warm chorizo.

Serves 4

Pickled pumpkin

1 cup superfine sugar

generous 3/4 cup good-quality red wine vinegar

1 (750-ml) bottle medium-dry white wine

3 bay leaves

2 tsp coriander seeds

1 tsp fennel seeds

small bunch of lemon thyme (or regular thyme)

1 fresh red chile

1 small pumpkin, or butternut squash, 3 to 4 1/2 pounds

Salad

small bunch of marjoram or oregano, leaves only

sea salt and freshly ground black pepper

few drops of lemon juice

1/4 cup extra virgin olive oil

12 slices of pickled pumpkin

8 slow-roasted tomato halves (page 123)

1 Burrata or fresh mozzarella ball

4 tsp aged balsamic vinegar

For the pickled pumpkin, put all the ingredients except the pumpkin into a heavy-bottomed wide pan. Place over low heat to allow the sugar to dissolve, stirring once or twice, then turn up the heat slightly to encourage the flavors to merge and get to know one another. Meanwhile, cut the pumpkin in half and scoop out the seeds, but leave the skin on. Slice the pumpkin into long fine wedges—the slices need to be thin to allow the sweet pickling flavor to permeate right through.

Place the pumpkin slices in the simmering pickling liquid. Turn down the heat as low as possible and poach very gently for 45 minutes until the pumpkin is tender to the bite—it should taste sweet and sour. Let cool in the syrup, then lift out the pickled pumpkin slices and pack into sterilized jars. Strain the pickling liquor and pour over the pumpkin. Seal and store in a cool dark place or the refrigerator—it will last for up to a good few weeks.

For the salad, using a mortar and pestle, gently pound the herb leaves with a small pinch of salt to a rough paste. Sprinkle over the lemon juice, add the olive oil, and stir well to combine. Taste the dressing for seasoning, adding a little pepper.

Arrange the pumpkin slices and slow-roasted tomatoes on serving plates and spoon the Burrata on top (if using mozzarella, tear it into pieces and place on top). Drizzle the herb dressing over the salad and around the plate. Trickle over the balsamic vinegar and serve.

The pumpkin I use for this recipe is the thin gray-skinned variety called Queensland blue, which has a pleasing texture when cooked. Butternut squash will work well, too.

Pan-fried mackerel with red wine vinegar, horseradish, and crème fraîche

Mackerel is a beautiful rich, oily fish that needs to be eaten very fresh to be fully enjoyed. The sharpness of the vinegar helps to cut the richness, and the heat of the horseradish and soft, sweet-sour flavor of crème fraîche make this a lovely dish. Serve it with some warm little potatoes that have been dressed with olive oil and sprinkled with chopped Italian parsley, or, as I do in the summer, with a bowl of green beans.

Serves 4

4 medium or 8 small mackerel, cleaned, and filleted if preferred

3 tbsp olive oil

sea salt and freshly ground black pepper

Sauce

1¹/2-inch piece of fresh horseradish

2 tbsp red wine vinegar

1 cup crème fraîche

sea salt and freshly ground black pepper

When you are cooking fish,

avoid overcrowding the pan. Either cook the fish in batches or use two pans.

Start by making the sauce. Peel the horseradish and grate it as finely as possible. (Be careful though, as very fresh horseradish will make you cry!) Tip the grated horseradish into a bowl and pour on the vinegar. Stir well to combine. Fold in the crème fraîche and season generously with salt, but only the smallest pinch of pepper. Set aside while you cook the fish.

If leaving the fish whole, rinse the cavity and pat dry. Using a sharp knife, make 3 diagonal slits on both sides of each fish. Brush the fish with a little olive oil and season with salt and pepper. Heat a large pan over high heat. If you are cooking the fish filleted, season the skin side only and pour the oil into the pan rather than rub it over the fish.

When the pan is hot, lay the fish in the pan—fillets should be placed skin side down. Cook whole fish without moving for 3 minutes on one side, then turn the fish over and cook on the other side for 3 minutes. Cook fillets for 4 minutes only without turning—just allow the flesh to cook through the skin side for a more delicate texture. The skin should have turned from silver to almost bronze and be papery thin and just crisp.

Arrange the fish on warm plates. Spoon the horseradish sauce alongside and serve piping hot—the best way to enjoy oily fish.

Slow-cooked shoulder of lamb with red wine vinegar

Shoulder of lamb cooked in this way becomes meltingly soft and tender. The shoulder contains more fat than the leg, which gives the meat a sweeter, fuller flavor. Red wine vinegar helps to cut the richness, while giving the dish a deep, sharp yet mellow note. The addition of anchovy is a lovely way to add saltiness to slow-cooked dishes.

Serves 4 to 6

1 shoulder of lamb, bone in, 3 to 4^1/$_2$ pounds

sea salt and freshly ground black pepper

1 tbsp olive oil

2^1/$_4$ cups white wine

1 tsp fennel seeds

2 dried red chiles, roughly chopped

5 cloves garlic, peeled

bunch of sage

1 bay leaf

6 good-quality anchovy fillets, packed in oil

5 tbsp red wine vinegar

I add dried red chile early

on to many slow-cooked dishes, as it provides a warm undertone, lending a profoundly satisfying flavor. In contrast to fresh chiles, which give unquestionable heat to dishes, dried chiles provide only warmth.

Preheat the oven to 325°F (convection oven to 325°F). Using a small sharp knife, trim the lamb of most of its surface fat, then season the meat liberally all over with salt and pepper. Place a large skillet (big enough to hold the lamb shoulder) on the stove over medium heat. Add the olive oil and when the pan is really hot, put in the lamb shoulder. Brown the meat well on all sides, turning as necessary; it will take about 10 minutes to achieve a good color all over.

Transfer the meat to a roasting pan and pour off the fat from the skillet. Return the skillet to low heat and pour in the wine. Let it bubble and reduce for a couple of minutes, then pour over the lamb.

Toast the fennel seeds in a dry pan until fragrant. Add to the roasting pan along with the chiles, garlic, sage, bay leaf, anchovies, and vinegar. Cover the roasting pan with foil, sealing it tightly around the edges. Cook on the middle shelf of the oven until the lamb is tender, 2^1/$_2$ to 3 hours.

Take the lamb out of the oven and remove the foil. Return to the oven and cook until the meat is very soft and wonderfully brown, 20 to 30 minutes. Taste the sauce for seasoning and adjust if necessary—it should be mellow, but rich and satisfying in flavor. I often serve this dish with farro or little white beans, but potatoes would be good, too.

Garlic

I find that almost everyone is seduced by the sweet smell of garlic cooking. As it emanates from the kitchen, the aroma draws you in, making you feel hungry. It is perhaps the most alluring of all smells, but to describe it is almost impossible. It is pungent, earthy, and powerful most certainly, but also subtle and delicate.

Garlic has been grown since time immemorial and has a place in culinary, medicinal, and religious contexts of almost all civilizations—ancient as well as modern. Varieties range from the smaller purple-tinged Italian and Spanish bulbs to big elephant garlic, which is very mild.

We tend to associate garlic with strength and punch, but it can be used delicately in dishes, too. Generally, the more garlic is pounded or chopped, the stronger the taste.

I rarely add garlic at the start of cooking, preferring to add it later—sometimes halfway through, but certainly after base flavoring ingredients such as onions, celery, and carrots. The result is a fuller, softer, more satisfying flavor.

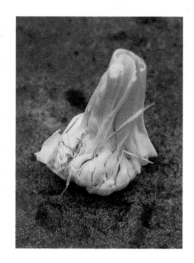

Garlic is harvested in late spring and early summer. I always look forward to a new season's spring garlic, with its long green stalk and lovely rose-tinged creamy bulb, all encased in fine, papery ivory skin. At this time of year, the individual cloves are not yet fully formed, and the immature papery layers in between them are completely edible. I like to braise the soft heads whole in stock or wine to enjoy their sweet, tender flesh.

Garlic can also be grown at home. Try planting a single clove (or a handful) in your garden in the fall, and come spring—if you are lucky—young green shoots will begin to appear. These shoots are good to eat too—lightly sautéed or added to salads.

◊

Wild garlic, which is also available in the spring, is quite different. It has fragrant, long, flat dark green leaves, but no bulb. You'll most likely come across it in damp woodlands or along riverbanks. Look for bluebells—the chances are wild garlic will be growing alongside. I simply wash the leaves and toss them quickly in a pan with a little oil or butter to serve alongside lamb or with the first of the season's wild salmon.

◊

When buying garlic, look for bulbs that are tight, firm, and hard, without any discoloration or bruises. If you've ever eaten a clove that is discolored and soft, you will not have forgotten its rancid taste and smell. Damaged cloves can spoil the taste of a cooked dish, so be sure to discard them. Store garlic bulbs in a cool, dry place, with good air circulation (not the refrigerator). Do not use garlic that has developed small green shoots. Also, if garlic is to be eaten raw, the central green shoot running through the middle of the clove should be removed, as it is indigestible.

◊

Aïoli is a pungent, garlicky sauce, which is delicious served alongside simply poached fish or broiled shellfish or stirred into seafood stews at the last minute. It is also lovely with raw tender young vegetables or a salad of sliced ripe tomatoes and green beans.

Aïoli My version is more gentle than the classic rustic Provençal sauce prepared from stale bread, garlic, and olive oil. To make it, pound 6 peeled garlic cloves to a paste with 1/2 tsp salt, using a mortar and pestle. In a bowl, beat 2 organic egg yolks with the pounded garlic and the juice of 1/2 lemon to combine. Measure a generous 1 cup mild-tasting extra virgin olive oil. Slowly begin to incorporate the oil into the garlicky base, drip by drip, whisking all the time. As the sauce begins to emulsify, you can add the oil a little more quickly. When it is all added, you should have a lovely thick garlicky mayonnaise—aïoli!

Baked garlic and shallots with fino

I make this dish in the spring, when the new season's garlic arrives. Its soft cloves—encased in sweet papery casings—are gentle in flavor, and the heads can be roasted and eaten whole. They go beautifully with roasted shallots. Serve as I do, on broiled bread, with a spoonful or two of soft goat cheese, or as an accompaniment to simple roast chicken.

Serves 4

4 heads of new season's garlic

8 large shallots

sea salt and freshly ground black pepper

5 thyme sprigs

4 bay leaves

2 1/2 cups fresh chicken stock

3/4 cup fino sherry

4 tbsp butter, in pieces

2 ounces Parmesan, grated

Preheat the oven to 375°F (convection oven to 350°F). Slice the garlic heads in half horizontally and place in a roasting pan. Halve the shallots and slip off their outer skin. Add to the garlic, season with salt and pepper, and scatter over the thyme and bay. Bring the stock to a boil in a small pan, then pour over the garlic and shallots. Drizzle over the sherry.

Cover the pan tightly with foil and roast in the oven for 35 to 40 minutes. Remove the foil and return to the oven until the shallots and garlic are golden brown and the stock has reduced down and thickened, 10 to 15 minutes. Add the butter and Parmesan and stir to combine. Taste and adjust the seasoning, then serve.

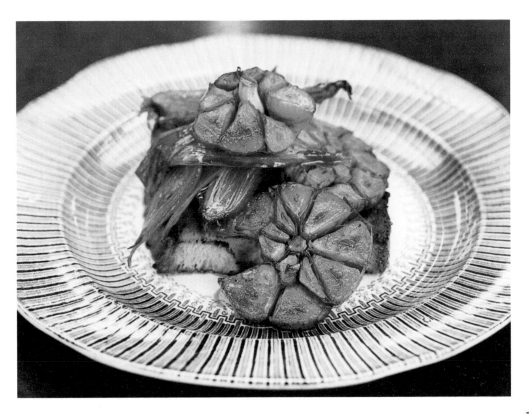

Fried egg with sage, chile, and garlicky yogurt

The combination of garlic, yogurt, and olive oil is irresistible. I use it not only for this dish, but also with perfectly ripe sweet tomatoes; with grated cucumber to make tzatziki; with roasted chicken; or simply on toast. You could poach the eggs if you prefer, but I think the crispy bits of the fried egg taste particularly good with the brown butter and creamy yogurt.

Serves 4

generous 1 cup good-quality strained plain yogurt (thick and only mildly sharp)

2 cloves garlic, peeled and crushed

sea salt

1/4 cup extra virgin olive oil

6 1/2 tbsp unsalted butter

8 sage leaves

4 very fresh organic eggs

1 fresh red chile, very finely sliced into rings (seeds left in)

Put the yogurt into a bowl with the garlic, a good pinch of salt, and the olive oil. Stir well to combine, taste, and add a little more salt if necessary. Set aside to let the flavors adjust to each other while you brown the butter.

Place the butter in a nonstick pan along with the sage over medium heat. Cook, stirring gently, until the butter begins to separate firstly, and then brown. The sediment at the bottom will taste nutty and delicious. You can strain it to remove the sediment if you like, but I prefer to leave it in. Set aside in a warm place while you cook the eggs.

Place one large (or two) nonstick skillet(s) over medium heat. Add a teaspoon of the browned butter, without the nutty sediment, to each skillet. When hot, crack the eggs into the skillets and add the sliced chile. Cook until the whites are firm and the yolks are soft. I like to spoon the hot butter over the whites to encourage the eggs to cook more quickly and to flavor them.

To serve, divide the garlicky yogurt among four plates, carefully lay the eggs on top, and scatter over the chile. Spoon the warm sage butter over the eggs and serve at once.

Very fresh eggs have bright, shiny yolks that sit proudly on top of bouncy, thick whites as you crack them into the pan. Thin, runny whites are an indication that the eggs are less than fresh.

Chicken with garlic and fennel

This is the sort of food I cook at home—quick, simple, and satisfying. During the summer, I'll most likely serve it with a plate of green beans and new potatoes from the garden, drizzled with peppery extra virgin olive oil.

Serves 4

1 organic chicken, about 3 pounds, jointed into 8 pieces

sea salt and freshly ground black pepper

2 tbsp olive oil

1 tsp fennel seeds

1 tsp coriander seeds

2 red onions, peeled and finely sliced

1 dried red chile

1 tsp saffron threads

4 cloves garlic, peeled and crushed

2 fennel bulbs, trimmed and fibrous outer layer removed

1 cup white wine

2 (12-ounce) cans good-quality peeled plum tomatoes

grated zest of 1 orange

3 bay leaves

5 thyme sprigs

1 or 2 tbsp extra virgin olive oil (optional)

Season the chicken well all over with salt and pepper. Put the olive oil in a Dutch oven or other heavy pot (large enough to hold all the ingredients comfortably) and place over medium heat. When hot, brown the chicken pieces in batches, turning to color them all over—they should look really golden and pleasing to the eye. Once browned, remove the pieces and set aside. Pour off any excess fat from the pot, leaving around 1 tbsp or so.

In a separate pan, gently warm the fennel and coriander seeds until they release their fragrance, then tip into a mortar and pound with the pestle to grind finely.

Add the onions to the pot and cook over low heat until sweet and translucent, about 5 minutes. Crumble over the chile and add the ground spices, saffron, and garlic. Season with a good pinch of salt and a little pepper, and stir well to combine. Cut the fennel bulb into quarters and add to the pot.

Pour in the wine, turn up the heat a little, and let bubble and reduce for a minute or so, then add the tomatoes. Return the chicken to the pot and add the orange zest and herbs. Turn down the heat and put the lid on the pot. Cook very gently for 40 minutes, or until the chicken is cooked through and almost starting to fall from the bone.

Taste and adjust the seasoning. If you're like me, you'll want to add a splash of extra virgin olive oil to bring the whole dish together. Serve with bread—or something else to mop up the delicious juices.

A dish such as this often tastes even better if left to cool to room temperature before reheating to serve. The flavors somehow adjust, get to know each other, and are that much better for it.

Good-quality pork is essential for this dish. We use a variety of pig known as Middlewhite, which is small in stature with sweet flesh—particularly that of the female. Male flesh invariably tastes a little stronger.

Slow-roasted pork flank with broccoli and puréed garlic

I love the creamy, smooth, and ever-so-slightly-pungent garlic purée that you find in Middle Eastern restaurants. Having never managed to persuade anyone to give me the recipe, I decided to come up with my own. It's really not bad and goes beautifully with the sweet, succulent flesh of pork flank. I find the crunchy crackling—achieved by cooking the pork in this way—totally irresistible.

Serves 6 to 8

4¹/2 pounds pork flank, with skin on and ribs intact

¹/4 cup olive oil

sea salt and freshly ground black pepper

1 tbsp fennel seeds

4 carrots, peeled and cut into chunks

4 celery stalks, cut into chunks

2 red onions, peeled and roughly chopped

3 bay leaves

few rosemary sprigs

2 dried red chiles

2 cups white wine

Garlic purée

20 very fresh cloves garlic, peeled but left whole

generous ³/4 cup milk

3 sprigs of lemon thyme (or ordinary thyme)

sea salt and freshly ground black pepper

¹/4 cup mild-tasting extra virgin olive oil

lemon juice

Broccoli

1¹/2 pounds broccoli or Broccolini, trimmed

2¹/2 tbsp extra virgin olive oil

1 fresh red chile, sliced (optional)

Preheat the oven to 400°F (convection oven to 400°F). Using a very sharp knife, score the skin of the pork at regular intervals, making the cuts about ¹/4 inch deep. Rub the olive oil into the flesh and season well all over with 1 tbsp sea salt and the fennel seeds. Place the pork flank, skin side up, in a roasting pan and roast on the middle shelf of the oven until the skin begins to blister and color and the crackling begins to form, 35 to 45 minutes.

Carefully lift out the pork onto a platter and scatter the vegetables, herbs, and dried chiles in the roasting pan. Pour over the wine, season lightly, and stir to combine. Rest the pork on top of the vegetables and cover with foil. Lower the oven setting to 325°F. Return the pan to the oven and cook until the meat is meltingly tender, 1¹/2 to 2 hours. Remove the foil and cook, uncovered, for another 10 to 20 minutes.

While the pork is roasting, make the garlic purée. Put the garlic, milk, and thyme sprigs in a small pan over gentle heat. Add a pinch of salt and bring to just under a simmer, then turn down the heat to very low and poach the garlic very gently until soft, about 35 minutes. The garlic should be very soft and almost falling apart. Using a slotted spoon, transfer the garlic cloves to a bowl and add a tablespoonful or so of the milk. Using a fork, mash to a purée, then stir in the olive oil. Add a few drops of lemon juice and season with a little more salt and pepper to taste; keep warm.

When the pork is ready, set aside to rest while you cook the broccoli. Add to a pan of boiling salted water and cook for about 3 minutes. Drain and immediately dress with the olive oil and chile.

Cut the pork into 3/4- to 1¹/4-inch-thick slices, sliding out the bones as you do so and discarding the vegetables. Arrange on warm plates with the broccoli. Spoon over the garlic purée and serve.

Stracotto

Known as *stracotto* in Tuscany and *brasato* in Piedmont, this delectable, melt-in-the-mouth dish is soft enough to eat with a spoon. I cook it every year, when the weather turns cooler and my thoughts turn to food that will nourish and sustain me. Rich and simple, this dish is the sum of its parts—good wine, a good but not expensive cut of meat, some aromatic herbs, and patience—the most invaluable ingredient of all. It will take all day to cook—but then good things come to those who wait.

Serves 6

3 to 4 1/2 pounds piece of chuck roast, trimmed of most (but not all) of its fat

sea salt and freshly ground black pepper

3 tbsp olive oil

3 yellow onions, peeled and chopped

4 carrots, peeled and roughly chopped

4 celery stalks, trimmed and chopped

10 cloves garlic, peeled but left whole

sprig of bay leaves (4 to 6 leaves)

small bunch of thyme sprigs

small bunch of Italian parsley

4 cups good-quality chicken stock

1 (750-ml) bottle red wine, preferably Chianti or Barbaresco

1 pig's foot (optional)

Season the meat generously all over with salt and pepper, then form into a neat roll and tie with string.

Heat the olive oil in a Dutch oven or other heavy pot (large enough to hold all the ingredients comfortably) over medium-high heat. When it is hot, add the meat and brown well all over, turning as necessary; this will take about 15 minutes. Lift out onto a plate and set aside.

Add the vegetables to the pot with the garlic and herbs, and turn down the heat slightly. Cook over fairly low heat for 15 minutes until the vegetables are soft and sweet.

Return the meat to the pot, pour over the stock and wine, and add the pig's foot. Put the lid on and reduce the heat to low. Cook over very low heat (use a heat diffuser if possible) for 5 hours. Remove the meat and bay leaves, then strain the sauce through a colander, pressing firmly with the back of a ladle to pass the vegetables through—this will thicken and enrich the final sauce.

Return the meat and bay leaves to the pot and pour over the strained sauce. Cook over very low heat for another hour. At this point, turn off the heat and let cool. (The flavor will be improved if the dish is left to come to room temperature and reheated to serve.)

Before serving, reheat the *stracotto* gently—the meat should now be falling apart, with a rich, glossy sauce to accompany it. Serve in warm soup plates, with whatever you like. We sometimes serve it with coarse yellow polenta, or cavolo nero, or just a salad of winter greens and good bread with which to mop up the juices.

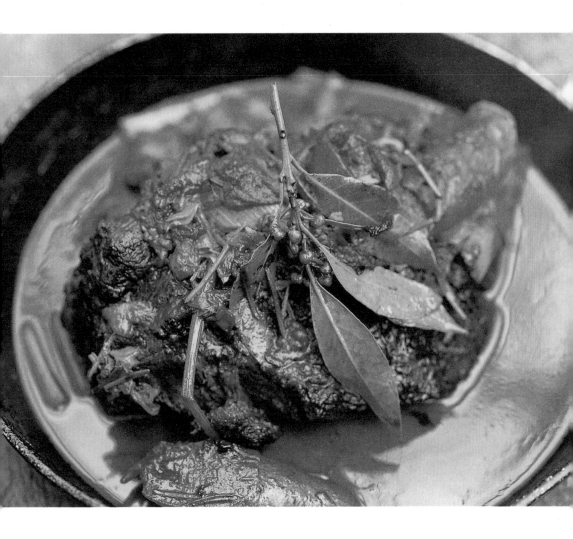

Game birds

Feathered game, in all its manifestations, tastes of the land on which it lived and fed. It has a mossy, woodland flavor with all the complexities that the particular landscape offers, but it is also majestic and glorious. I associate game strongly with England and, more broadly, Europe. It reminds me of fresh air, sport, a big hunger, and deep robust red wines. Without a doubt, it becomes very much central stage in any dish.

The beauty of game is that each variety has a unique, deep, and satisfying flavor, providing nuances of taste that are not found in other meats—the delicate slightly livery taste of squab, for example, or the musty earthy taste of grouse. Game works beautifully with the fall's bounty of produce—wild mushrooms, root vegetables, nuts, Brussels sprouts and other brassicas, delicate cauliflower, even pomegranates, and quince. Game offers so many possibilities that I'm always eager for the start of the season when the first grouse appear.

Careful thought and consideration is needed when pairing game with other ingredients. Understandably, bread very often features—in the form of bread crumbs or bread sauce—as it provides a foil for game meats that have a very strong taste. Grouse, perhaps the most intensely flavored of all the birds, certainly benefits from this coupling and I often serve it on toast. All game, though very different in taste, has a sense of woodland about it—moss, berries, mushrooms, and so on—so these flavors also complement the birds in cooking. The delicate, earthy characteristics of chanterelles and porcini, for example, work well with partridge, mallard, and quail.

Strictly speaking, quail and guinea fowl are classified as poultry rather than game these days, as they are now protected species in the UK. Those that you buy will probably have been farmed, hence their milder taste. As with chicken, seek out organic birds for optimum flavor.

◊

Game often has a dark appearance and a very strong smell because it has been hung, but you need to be assured that it is in good condition for eating. The fat should be creamy and fairly intact, and the aroma should be decent, albeit strong. Always check game birds for shot, too, as the resulting damage can give the meat a taste of metal. Also, torn flesh can dry and harden around the edges—cooking will not improve or mask this damage.

I strongly recommend that you look for a reputable game dealer or butcher, who deals with small hunters and suppliers. Our game dealer, Albert, or "Albert the Grouseman" as we call him, has dealt in game for many years and always brings us only the very best of what he can lay his hands on. A one-man band, his produce never disappoints.

Like Albert, I believe it is best to wait until there is something really good and worthy of cooking than to eat game in less than perfect condition. Our game arrives plucked, hung, and ready to eat. We give it a quick wipe over with a clean damp cloth and place it in a sealed large plastic container with space and air surrounding it, then store it in the refrigerator and cook within a few days of purchase.

Never has nature seemed more noble or majestic than in the lay of the feathers of game birds. Soft like velvet, with both vibrant and muted hues—of amber, rust, chocolate, and blue—man could not have created anything quite like this beauty.

Guinea fowl supremes with braised tardivo and balsamic mayonnaise

I am very fond of guinea fowl as it has a gentle taste—no more intense than properly flavored chicken—and because it was one of my father's favorite things to eat, so it always reminds me of him. Like round radicchio, elongated tardivo is delicious broiled, turning bittersweet as it slightly chars—this flavor works well with all game birds. The mayonnaise accompanying the dish is caramely, rich, and elegant; it complements the tender meat perfectly.

Serves 4

1 large head of tardivo or round radicchio

¹/4 cup extra virgin olive oil

sea salt and freshly ground black pepper

3 tbsp aged balsamic vinegar

4 guinea fowl supremes (bone-in, skin-on breasts with the first wing joint attached)

1 to 2 tbsp olive oil, for cooking

Balsamic mayonnaise

3 organic egg yolks

sea salt

¹/2 tbsp Dijon mustard

1 tbsp lemon juice

generous 1 cup mild-tasting extra virgin olive oil

2 tbsp aged balsamic vinegar

First make the mayonnaise. Whisk the egg yolks with a pinch of salt, then whisk in the mustard and lemon juice. Trickle in the olive oil, very slowly to begin with, whisking constantly, then more steadily once the sauce begins to emulsify. Continue until all the oil is incorporated. Stir in the vinegar and set aside to let the flavors become acquainted, while you cook the dish.

Preheat the broiler. To prepare the tardivo, remove any wilted or damaged leaves, then slice vertically into 1¹/2-inch wedges so that the leaves are still attached to the core. Toss in a bowl with the extra virgin olive oil to coat and season with salt. Let stand for a minute or two, to allow the oil to soften the leaves slightly.

Place the tardivo, cut side down, on the broiler rack and cook until slightly charred at the edges. Turn and cook for about 3 minutes on the other side. Don't be tempted to prod it during cooking; as the outer leaves char, the inner ones will soften, becoming sweet and tender. Dress, while still warm, with the vinegar.

To cook the guinea fowl, preheat the oven to 425°F (convection oven to 425°F). Season the birds generously with salt and pepper. Place a large, heavy ovenproof skillet (preferably nonstick) over fairly high heat. When the skillet is smoking hot, add the olive oil, then brown the guinea fowl in batches. Lay 2 supremes in the skillet, skin side down, and cook without moving for about 3 minutes. Remove to a warm plate and repeat with the other 2 supremes, adding a little more oil if needed.

Return the first 2 supremes to the skillet, skin side down, then place the skillet in the oven for 4 to 8 minutes to finish cooking the guinea fowl—the skin will be very crisp and the flesh should be firm, succulent, and tender. Set aside to rest for 5 minutes.

Warm the tardivo if necessary and serve with the guinea fowl. Pass the mayonnaise separately so everyone can help themselves.

Grilled partridge with chile, marjoram, and ricotta

This is a slightly surprising but delicious way to treat partridge. Instead of being paired in the usual manner with rich wine, nuts, mushrooms, or bread, here it is spiked with the clean, vibrant flavors of marjoram, chile, and lemon juice. This works particularly well with the slightly charred succulence of meat that has been cooked over an open fire. Very fresh sheep's milk ricotta rounds the dish off with a delicate sweetness.

Serves 4

4 partridges, plucked and cleaned, but not trussed

sea salt and freshly ground black pepper

2 fresh red chiles, finely sliced

handful of marjoram sprigs, plus extra leaves to finish

1 lemon, halved

5 tbsp very good extra virgin olive oil

8 thin slices of pancetta

4 slices of crusty, white peasant-style bread

scant 1 cup fresh ricotta, or other soft curd cheese

lemon wedges, to serve

Using poultry scissors, cut away the backbone of each partridge, to enable you to open the bird out. The easiest way to do this is to cut either side of the bone where the ribs join, then push the bird out flat with your open hand.

Put the birds into a large shallow dish. Season them with salt and pepper, and scatter over the chiles and marjoram sprigs. Squeeze over the lemon juice and drizzle with all but 1 tbsp of the olive oil. Turn the birds to coat once or twice, then let marinate for 30 minutes or so.

Heat up your grill or preheat the broiler or stovetop grill pan. When hot, lay the partridges, skin side down, on the rack or grill pan. Cook, turning frequently so that they brown and cook evenly all over, for about 25 minutes until the flesh is pink and tender, but not too rare. Remove to a warm plate and rest for 5 minutes.

In the meantime, cook the pancetta slices until slightly browned and toast the bread on the grill or grill pan. Place a slice of toast on each warm plate and drizzle with a little olive oil. Add a spoonful of ricotta and a slice of pancetta, then a scattering of marjoram leaves. Place a partridge on top and serve at once, with lemon wedges.

Partridges, like other game birds, are improved by an early salting, as this enhances their juiciness and texture and gives time for the seasoning to diffuse through the meat. Allow 1 tbsp of good-quality sea salt for each bird. Salt evenly all over and refrigerate for at least 24 hours. Wipe off any excess salt and do not reseason before cooking.

Wild duck with porcini and red wine

With the exception of confit, which I love to eat in the winter, I don't cook duck all that often. Duck breast cooked in the usual way does little for me. However, the young wild ducks that are around in the fall and early winter are altogether different. Small enough for one, their rich, tender flesh is lovely. Here I've matched them with fresh porcini and a simple red wine reduction. You might like to serve them with soft polenta. (Illustrated on previous page.)

Serves 4

4 small, young wild ducks, plucked and cleaned

1/2 cup plus 1 tbsp unsalted butter

sea salt and freshly ground black pepper

9 ounces fresh porcini mushrooms (if unavailable use 2 ounces dried porcini)

1 (750-ml) bottle good-quality red wine

few rosemary sprigs

1 clove garlic, peeled and crushed

Preheat the oven to 400°F (convection oven to 400°F). Wash the ducks and pat dry. Now butterfly them: Cut down either side of the backbone, then open the birds out and press down with the heel of your hand to flatten. Smear a small piece of butter over the breast of each bird (use two-thirds of the butter) and season generously all over.

To prepare the fresh porcini, carefully scrape away any dirt with a knife, then wipe them with a damp cloth. Cut them in half lengthwise and check there are no worms. Remove any damaged bases from the caps, but do not discard them. (If using dried porcini, soak in hot water for about 15 minutes. Remove the mushrooms and set aside; strain the liquor through a fine strainer and reserve.)

Pour the red wine into a wide pan and add the rosemary sprigs and trimmed mushroom bases (or reserved soaking liquor). Bring to a simmer over medium heat and let bubble until reduced by almost half; strain and set aside.

Place the ducks in a roasting pan, but don't overcrowd the pan (use two pans if necessary). Place on the middle shelf of the oven and roast for 15 to 20 minutes, basting halfway through cooking. This timing will give you beautifully cooked birds, but you can always allow a few minutes longer if you like, or a few minutes less if you prefer the meat rare. Set aside in a warm place to rest.

Place a nonstick skillet over medium-high heat and add the remaining 3 tbsp butter. When it is foaming, throw in the porcini caps and garlic, and season with a little salt and pepper. Cook undisturbed for a minute, then turn and cook on the other side for a couple of minutes. The porcini should have taken on a wonderful color around the edges. Pour in the reduced wine and cook for another 5 minutes.

Place a duck on each warm plate and spoon the porcini and sauce over. Serve at once.

Roasted quail with chanterelles and spinach

Delicate little quail may offer you no more than five or six mouthfuls each, but their flesh has such a delightful sweet, nutty flavor that I adore eating them. Chanterelles—pan-fried with a little garlic and tossed with spinach leaves—make a wonderful and natural partner.

Serves 4

8 quails

7 ounces chanterelles

1 pound 2 ounces young spinach

1/2 cup unsalted butter

sea salt and freshly ground black pepper

1 clove garlic, peeled and minced

lemon juice

Preheat the oven to 400°F (convection oven to 400°F). Wash the quails and pat dry. Wipe the chanterelles with a clean, soft, damp cloth to remove any dirt (never rinse them, as you will wash away their gentle flavor). Wash the spinach thoroughly under cold running water, then drain in a colander.

Place a small piece of butter inside the cavity of each bird, then smear a little over the breasts (use about half of the butter). Season generously with salt and pepper. Place the quails in a roasting pan on the middle shelf of the oven and roast until the breasts are firm to the touch, 8 to 15 minutes.

While the quails are cooking, cook the spinach in batches if necessary. Simply place it in a dry pan with only the water clinging to the leaves after washing and cook briefly over medium heat until just wilted. Drain in a colander and leave until cool enough to handle, then squeeze with your hands to remove excess water and set aside while you cook the chanterelles. Once the quails are cooked, set them aside to rest in a warm place.

To cook the chanterelles, place a nonstick skillet over fairly high heat. Once the skillet is hot, add a third of the remaining butter and let it sizzle slightly, then add the chanterelles and season lightly with salt and pepper. Let cook for a couple of minutes—don't prod or poke them as this encourages them to release moisture and can ruin their final texture.

Now add the garlic and spinach to the chanterelles and stir to heat the spinach and mingle the flavors. Add the rest of the butter, a good squeeze of lemon juice, and a grinding of black pepper.

Serve the spinach and chanterelles piping hot alongside the quail.

Squab with cranberry beans and cavolo

In this recipe I have used dried cranberry beans, which are different from the beautiful cranberry beans we grow in our vegetable garden in the summer. The dried beans are heavier and less creamy, but delicious with cavolo nero, Tuscany's black leaf kale—and perfect with roasted squab.

Serves 4

4 squabs (young pigeons), plucked and cleaned, but not trussed

olive oil, to drizzle

sea salt and freshly ground black pepper

Cranberry beans

2 1/2 cups dried cranberry beans, soaked overnight

1 (12-ounce) can good-quality peeled plum tomatoes, chopped

1 small bunch of sage

1 head of garlic, halved crosswise

1 dried red chile

sea salt

1/2 cup extra virgin olive oil

Cavolo nero

1 pound 2 ounces cavolo nero

about 3 tbsp extra virgin olive oil

4 tbsp unsalted butter

2 cloves garlic, peeled and minced

4 good-quality canned anchovy fillets in olive oil, drained

1/2 dried red chile

sea salt and freshly ground black pepper

First prepare the cranberry beans. Drain the beans and put them into a large, heavy cooking pot. Cover generously with cold water, but do not season. Add the tomatoes, sage, and garlic, then crumble over the chile. Bring to a boil over medium heat, then turn down the heat and simmer until the beans are tender to the bite, about 45 minutes.

In the meantime, cook the squabs. Preheat the oven to 450°F (convection oven to 450°F). Place the squabs in a lightly oiled roasting pan, season them well all over and inside the cavity with salt and pepper, and drizzle with a little olive oil. Place in the hot oven and roast for 10 to 20 minutes, depending on size, until tender. When cooked, set aside to rest in a warm place for 10 minutes.

When the cranberry beans are cooked, season them with a good pinch of salt. Drain and dress, while warm, with the olive oil. Set aside while you cook the cavolo nero.

Bring a large pan of well-salted water to a boil. Wash the cavolo leaves and strip them from their woody central stalks. Once the water is boiling vigorously, plunge in the cavolo leaves and cook for 2 to 3 minutes until tender to the bite. Drain in a colander and dress, while warm, with the olive oil.

Place half of the cavolo in a blender with the butter, garlic, anchovies, and chile. Purée until smooth, adding a little more olive oil if the mixture is too thick—it should be inky black, glossy, and smooth. Season to taste with salt and a little pepper.

Return the purée to the pan and stir in the whole cavolo nero leaves and cranberry beans. Warm through and serve piping hot alongside the roasted squab.

Roasted grouse with Barolo on toast

The ideal size for one, grouse have a particular deep, rich, complex flavor and, when properly cooked, they are perfectly tender. Here I've served them simply with a rich wine sauce, made from Italian Barolo, and crunchy, yet slightly sodden toast—if that makes any sense.

Serves 4

4 grouse, plucked and cleaned, but not trussed

generous 2/3 cup unsalted butter

small bunch of thyme

sea salt and freshly ground black pepper

4 slices of chewy peasant-style bread

4 fresh porcini or portobello mushrooms, cleaned and thickly sliced

handful of tardivo or roughly torn round radicchio leaves

handful of frisée

olive oil

lemon juice

13/4 cups Barolo wine

1 tbsp minced parsley, to serve

Preheat the oven to 450°F (convection oven to 450°F). Wash the birds and pat dry. Place 4 tsp of the butter in a Dutch oven or other heavy pot and melt slowly over gentle heat on the stove top. Divide the thyme in four and insert a portion into the cavity of each bird. Place a piece of butter inside each bird and smear more butter over the breasts, reserving 4 tbsp to cook the porcini and finish the sauce. Season the birds generously with salt and pepper.

Place the grouse in the cooking pot and put on the middle shelf of the oven. Roast for 7 to 10 minutes, then remove from the oven and baste in the now-foaming butter.

Place a slice of bread under each grouse and return to the oven for about 5 minutes to finish cooking the birds and effectively cook the bread. The bread will not only crisp up, but also absorb all the lovely flavors of the grouse. The skin of the grouse should be crisp and, when pressed with your finger, the flesh should be bouncy and firm.

In the meantime, melt half the remaining butter in a skillet. When foaming, add the mushrooms and season with a little salt and pepper. Cook, turning occasionally, until tender.

Dress the salad leaves with a little olive oil and lemon juice, and season lightly with salt and pepper.

Transfer the grouse and toast to a warm platter; keep warm. Place the pot on the stove top over high heat and pour in the wine, stirring to deglaze. Let bubble until reduced by half, swirling the pot every now and then to gather up all the tasty pan juices.

Arrange the birds on toast on individual plates. Add the final piece of butter to the wine reduction, stirring vigorously as it melts into the sauce. Taste and add a little salt and pepper if required, then spoon over the birds. Pile the salad leaves and mushrooms on top and sprinkle with the minced parsley. Serve at once.

Apples

The English have long loved the cultivation and eating of apples—almost two and a half thousand different varieties have been grown in the UK at one time or another. My thoughts always turn to them come early September, though in truth apples are in season in the UK from July until early March. During July and August, like everyone else, I become immersed in the abundance of summer fruit in season—soft ripe berries, cherries, peaches, nectarines, and juicy orange-fleshed melons from Italy—anxious not to miss out on any of them. It is without doubt the best time of the year for fruit and so, sadly, I tend to overlook apples.

However, as soon as September arrives and the weather gradually begins to turn cooler, I find myself thinking about apples—all the different varieties with their beautiful colors, flavors, and textures—and how I can use them in the kitchen.

At one time, apple orchards in England were as important to the landscape—and to the people who tended them and cooked with their produce—as vineyards are to the French and olive groves are to the Italians. In essence, they have contributed to England's historical identity. Sadly, these days we see few varieties, because supermarkets and most food outlets concentrate on selling those apples that are easiest to grow and have long shelf lives—many flown in from halfway across the world. No longer are beautiful English varieties with intriguing names such as Cox's Orange Pippin, Laxton's Fortune, Cornish Gillyflower, and Pitmaston Pine familiar to all.

◊

Each year at Petersham we celebrate Apple Day on October 21. This year we made toffee apples and old-fashioned tomato and apple ketchup to sell in the café. We also slow-cooked suckling pig and served it warm, wrapped in sourdough bread with apple sauce. Wendy, who I work with, stayed up long into the night to reproduce a Victorian board game, rather like snakes and ladders—for children to play on tables in the café in between bobbing for apples. Brogdale and Chegworth Valley farms in Kent supplied us with rare breed apples to sell. As we laid these out on a long table for comparison, the different varieties simply took our breath away—their forms, colors, and aromas are so diverse.

◊

Apples are wonderful combined in salads with nuts, sharp cheeses, and gentle sweet lettuces. They are also excellent paired with cabbage, the last of the summer's tomatoes, sweet crabmeat, or young pork. And, of course, apples lend themselves to all manner of spicy chutneys and jellies, warm tarts, desserts, and refreshing sorbets and ice creams. The possibilities are endless.

When it comes to choosing apples, opt for those that feel firm and heavy for their size. They should be free of blemishes and have a fresh aroma. Try to seek out the more unusual varieties, too. Begin by asking your greengrocer or local farmers' market for particular varieties when they are ready for picking. Support local growers who sell a wider range of varieties and, through exploration, discover the myriad and wonderful possibilities of taste that apples can provide.

A good apple is full of character and its mere appearance can make you smile. I love the individual characteristics and particular colors of apples. Their imperfections are to be embraced and enjoyed. Of all the varieties, it is crisp, tart apples that I use most frequently—in salads and desserts, including baking.

Apple, fennel, smoky ham, and hazelnut salad

This crisp, crunchy salad is perfect for late summer or early fall. The combination of sweet apple, peppery kohlrabi, crunchy fennel, and smoky ham is truly delicious. Speck, a distinctive cured ham flavored with juniper, is particularly good in this salad. Hazelnuts are a lovely addition, or you could use cobnuts instead when they come into season.

Serves 4

scant 1/2 cup hazelnuts

2 crisp apples

juice of 1/2 lemon

1 fennel bulb

1 kohlrabi bulb

6 large radicchio leaves

sea salt and freshly ground black pepper

4 tsp olive oil

8 very thin slices of speck or prosciutto

1 tbsp minced parsley

Dressing

1 organic egg yolk

1 tsp Dijon mustard

1 tsp honey

1 tbsp cider vinegar

sea salt and freshly ground black pepper

1/3 cup mild-tasting extra virgin olive oil

2 tsp crème fraîche

Preheat the oven to 375°F (convection oven to 350°F). For the dressing, put the egg yolk in a bowl and add the mustard, honey, vinegar, and some salt and pepper. Whisk to combine, then very slowly pour in the olive oil, whisking as you do so, until it is all added and the dressing is combined. Stir in the crème fraîche and set aside.

Scatter the hazelnuts on a roasting pan and lightly toast them in the oven for 2 to 4 minutes. Remove and let cool slightly, then rub in a cloth to remove the skins and chop roughly.

For the salad, core the apples and slice into fine discs, leaving the skins on. Toss with half of the lemon juice to prevent browning. Remove the tougher outer layer from the fennel and slice into rounds. Peel the kohlrabi and cut into fine discs. Sprinkle the rest of the lemon juice over the fennel and kohlrabi. Wash the radicchio leaves, pat dry, and cut into ribbons.

To assemble, put the fennel, kohlrabi, radicchio, and apple slices in a bowl. Season with a little salt and pepper and drizzle over the olive oil. Toss together lightly with your fingertips.

Divide the salad among serving plates. Arrange the speck slices on top, drizzle over the dressing, and finish with the chopped nuts and parsley. Serve at once.

Kohlrabi, apple, and crab salad

Kohlrabi is an underrated vegetable that deserves more recognition. I find its clean, slightly peppery taste irresistible, especially when eaten raw, finely sliced in a salad, perhaps because it is a little like cabbage in flavor. Here it works beautifully with thinly sliced apple and fresh white crabmeat.

Serves 4

1 kohlrabi

1 crisp apple

7 ounces fresh white crabmeat

handful of curly parsley, stalks removed, leaves minced

2 tbsp extra virgin olive oil

sea salt and freshly ground black pepper

2 to 3 perfectly ripe tomatoes, sliced

Dressing

1 organic egg yolk

1¹/₂ tsp honey

1 tsp Dijon mustard

1 tbsp cider vinegar

sea salt and freshly ground black pepper

generous ¹/₃ cup extra virgin olive oil

1 tbsp heavy cream

Peel the kohlrabi and slice as finely as possible. Core and slice the apple into fine discs, leaving the skin on. Place the kohlrabi and apple in a bowl, add the crabmeat, parsley, and olive oil, and season with a little salt and pepper. Toss together lightly with your fingers. Set aside while you make the dressing.

Place the egg yolk in a blender or small food processor and add the honey, mustard, vinegar, and a little salt and pepper. Whiz to combine, then, with the motor running, very slowly drizzle in the olive oil. When it is all incorporated, add the cream, turn off the motor, and pour the dressing into a bowl.

Layer the salad and tomato slices attractively on individual plates, spoon over a little of the dressing and serve right away. Pass the remaining dressing separately in a pitcher.

Crab and apple are a delicate combination... sweet and light as air, this salad needs to be dressed with a gentle hand as the flavors require subtlety to be fully appreciated.

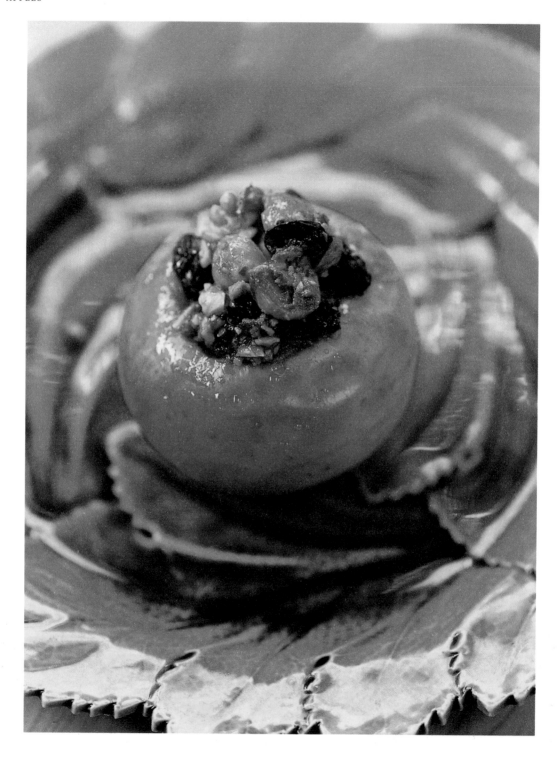

Little baked apples

I think of these cheery little apples as comfort food. I love their warmth and caramely, spicy richness. They are simple to make and you needn't be precise with the quantities—adjust the flavorings according to taste, perhaps adding a little chopped candied orange peel as I do.

Serves 4

4 crisp apples suitable for baking, such as Gala, Stayman, or Winesap

8 blanched almonds

2 tbsp apple brandy (or cognac or ordinary brandy)

1 tbsp dried currants

1 tbsp golden raisins

1 tbsp dark raisins

finely grated zest and juice of 1 orange

finely grated zest of 1 lemon

3 tbsp brown sugar

2 tbsp unsalted butter, melted

thick cream or vanilla ice cream (page 34), to serve

Preheat the oven to 375°F (convection oven to 350°F). Wash the apples and set aside. Warm the almonds on a baking sheet in the oven for just a few minutes.

Gently warm the brandy in a small pan over low heat. Put the currants, golden raisins, and dark raisins in a bowl, add the orange and lemon zests, and toss to mix. Pour over the orange juice and the warm brandy, stir to combine, and leave for a few minutes to let the warm alcohol plump up and soften the dried fruit.

Chop the nuts and add to the mixture with the sugar and butter. Stir well, then set aside while you prepare the apples.

Using a small sharp knife, remove a small slice from the base of each apple, so that they will sit happily on a baking sheet without rolling over. Hollow out the center of the apples, making sure that you don't cut right through to the base. Make two little cuts in the skin of each apple—this will help to deter the skin from splitting as the apples swell during cooking.

Spoon the filling into the apples and stand them on a baking sheet. Bake on the middle shelf of the oven until they are tender when pressed and the filling is oozing and bubbling, 15 to 25 minutes.

Remove from the oven and let stand for 5 minutes or so before serving—these little apples taste better served warm rather than piping hot. Pass the cream or ice cream separately.

Apple ice cream with toasted nuts and caramel sauce

I love the idea of apple ice cream, but many times I've been disappointed with the outcome, which often seems to taste a little too much like baby food for my liking. Determined to come up with an ice cream that tasted very clearly of apple with a clean, slightly lemony bite, I started experimenting. This is the result—I think it's really quite good.

Serves 4

5 crisp apples

juice of 1 lemon

2 tbsp apple brandy (or cognac)

3/4 cup superfine sugar

generous 2/3 cup heavy cream

Caramel sauce

1¹/4 cups sugar

¹/2 cup water

pinch of sea salt

generous 1 cup heavy cream

To serve

10 cobnuts or hazelnuts

Peel, quarter, and core the apples, then chop them into small pieces. Put into a blender with the lemon juice and whiz until smooth. Pour in the brandy, add the sugar, and blend again. Now pour in the cream and process briefly to combine the mixture. Taste—it should be sweet and boozy, but with a sharp, clean apple finish. Pour into an ice-cream maker and churn until thickened and set, following the manufacturer's instructions.

Preheat the oven to 375°F (convection oven to 350°F). Place the nuts on a baking sheet and roast in the oven until golden, 4 to 6 minutes. Tip onto a board and let cool, then chop roughly.

To make the caramel sauce, put the sugar and water into a small heavy pan over low heat to dissolve the sugar, stirring once. When dissolved, turn up the heat to medium and cook without stirring to a rich dark caramel—this may take up to 10 minutes.

As the caramel begins to turn golden brown, watch it carefully as it can burn quickly, but take it to a deep mahogany color (under-cooked caramel tastes insipid). Add the salt and remove from the heat. Immediately pour in the cream—standing well back and protecting your hand with an oven mitt as it tends to splutter. Once it has settled down, return to the heat and cook over low heat, stirring with a wooden spoon, for a minute or so. Remove from the heat and let cool.

To serve, scoop the ice cream into bowls, spoon over a little caramel sauce, and sprinkle with the toasted nuts. Serve immediately.

Apple galette

This is a lovely apple tart. The dough is flaky and crunchy and the topping of finely sliced apples is beautifully caramelized. I like to glaze the tart with a special grape jelly that we make in the early fall from *uva di fragola* (strawberry-scented grapes). It gives the tart the most beautiful purple hue and scented flavor, but you can use apple jelly instead, or simply leave the tart unglazed. This quantity of dough will make two tarts—it freezes well so I always make enough for another one.

Serves 8

Pie dough

1 pound 2 ounces all-purpose flour, plus extra to dust

1/2 tsp sea salt

1 tsp superfine sugar

13/4 cups butter, cut into 1/2-inch dice

1/2 cup ice water

Apple filling

21/4 pounds crisp apples

2 tbsp unsalted butter, melted

scant 1 cup superfine sugar

apple or grape jelly, warmed, to glaze (optional)

Very fine dough is divine with sweet, fragrant just-cooked apples. Cool, creamy vanilla ice cream (page 34) that just melts into the warm tart is what is called for here.

To make the dough, combine the flour, salt, and sugar in a large mixing bowl. Add 8 pieces of diced butter and lightly rub into the flour mixture with your fingertips until the mixture resembles coarse sand. Add the remaining butter dice and work together again lightly with your fingers just until the butter pieces are broken down. Large bits of butter make this dough really tender.

Now add the ice water in several stages, tossing the mixture together with your fingers until it just comes together. Don't pinch or squeeze the dough or you will overwork it. The dough will have some wetter patches and some dryer ones, which is fine. Cut the dough in half and shape each piece firmly into a ball. Wrap each ball tightly in waxed paper and flatten with the palm of your hand to a disc, about 3/4 inch thick. Refrigerate for 1 hour. Freeze one portion of dough to use for another tart.

Preheat the oven to 425°F (convection oven to 400°F). Unwrap the chilled dough and gently roll out on a lightly floured surface to a 9-inch circle, 1/4 inch thick. Transfer to a baking sheet. Quarter and core the apples, leaving the skins on, then slice thinly—the slices should only be 1/4 inch thick.

Starting about 1 inch in from the edge of the dough circle, arrange the apples, slightly overlapping, in concentric circles until you reach the center. Now pinch and twist the edge of the dough, rotating the tart as you do so, to create a border that resembles a twisted rope around the apples. Brush the melted butter gently over the apple slices and dough. Sprinkle 2 tbsp of the sugar over the dough border. Scatter the rest of the sugar over the apples.

Bake in the center of the oven for 30 to 40 minutes until the apples are soft and the crust is golden brown, rotating the tart 180 degrees after about 15 minutes to ensure it colors evenly. Let rest for 15 minutes, then brush with the warm jelly to glaze.

Cheese

From the beginning, I knew that the cheese course would be important to me at the restaurant; I was also sure that a large selection would not be right. I've always preferred to choose from a small, carefully considered menu, rather than one with endless options. So for the cheese course, one well-chosen cheese—served not with bread or cookies, but with natural seasonal partners —seemed perfect. I enjoy the challenge immensely. Finding the right firm, crunchy, sweet pear to accompany sharp, chalky romano for example; or fall raspberries and a little drizzle of our local honey to partner perfectly ripe creamy English Wigmore cheese. I love the process of tasting a new cheese… pausing, thinking, often rejecting, and discussing with others in the kitchen what works. It is a question of pairing textures as well as flavors, to showcase the beauty of not only the cheese, but also its companion.

Cheese, more than any other food, holds a sense of romance for me. It is so much a product of its terrain, flora, fauna, and clime, yet its unique attributes are also influenced by man. Some cheeses, like the Swiss vacherin, are purely seasonal; the characteristics of others change with the seasons. With so many different varieties, there is a myriad of tastes, textures, and aromas to experience.

I urge you to find a good cheese store close to you, peer in through the window, and see the magic inside. Try one or two cheeses you may have previously shied away from because their aroma seemed too strong or their names were unpronounceable or off-putting. Stinking bishop, for example, does smell overpowering but it is in fact a delicious, complex English cheese.

◊

When choosing cheese, look for signs that it has been respectfully handled. Each cheese is different of course, but there are certain common indicators. The cheese should not look overhandled, neither should it be oily or dry around the edges. Surprisingly, perhaps, mold on the rind of a hard cheese is often a good sign. Above all, a cheese should have a sense of freshness about it.

As for storage, this varies according to the type of cheese. I wrap hard cheeses in plastic wrap, leaving the crust to breathe. Soft cheeses are better wrapped in waxed paper, as are all blue cheeses. Goat cheeses should be kept loosely covered in the refrigerator. Never let cheeses sit uncovered in the refrigerator—the cold air will dry them out, and their flavor is easily tainted by other foods.

◊

Producers and suppliers who have a heartfelt connection with their products, the land, and the seasons are of the utmost importance to me. I learn from them and they help me to become a better cook. Patricia Michelson, owner of the Fromagerie, sources farmhouse cheeses directly from small artisan producers. Her energy, passion, and knowledge inspire me and her faultless palate always challenges mine!

If the idea of serving a very simple cheeseboard of one beautiful cheese with harmonizing partners appeals to you, then you might like to try some of the lovely pairings we have stumbled across:

Cheddar with raw fennel and crisp apple, such as Newtown Pippin.

Vacherin drizzled with the tiniest hint of walnut oil and warmed in the oven along with fresh walnuts (warmed in their shells).

Fourme d'Ambert with dried white figs pickled in red wine.

Young lemony goat cheeses with ripe apricots and slightly warm pecans.

◊

Using cheese in cooking is another skill. To ensure that a cheese maintains its inherent flavor and texture through the cooking process requires thought and attention. Certain cheeses, including Gruyère, fontina, raclette, and Comté, have a natural affinity with heat. Soft young, creamy cheeses work well in baking, but in truth, most cheeses are best enjoyed in their natural state.

Bruschetta of sheep's milk ricotta, lemon oil, and bresaola

Light-as-air ricotta is wonderful on broiled bread with thin slices of bresaola—a soft, sweet, air-dried cured beef from Italy. This soft sheep's milk cheese is also delicious for breakfast—with a spoonful of honey and perfectly ripe apricots or summer berries. In winter, I love to flavor it with pounded rosemary and a little dried chile to eat with marinated artichokes. It is a truly versatile cheese.

Serves 4

5 1/2 ounces sheep's milk ricotta or other soft curd cheese

finely grated zest of 1 lemon

4 slices of good-quality chewy, peasant-style bread, cut about 1/2 inch thick

1 clove garlic, peeled

3/8 cup lemon-infused olive oil (see page 63)

sea salt and freshly ground black pepper

8 thin slices of bresaola

Place the ricotta in a bowl, add the lemon zest, and fold together gently. Set aside.

Preheat the broiler and toast the slices of bread until golden brown on both sides. Once the bread is a really good color, remove from the broiler and rub gently with the garlic clove. Brush the garlicky bread with a little of the lemon-infused oil and season with a little salt.

Arrange a slice of bresaola on each bruschetta on each serving plate. Add a spoonful of ricotta, then top with a final slice of bresaola. Drizzle over a little lemon-infused oil. Finish with a sprinkling of salt and pepper and serve at once.

For bruschetta, the ideal bread

is an open-pored, well-textured loaf. We use pagnotta, which is baked for us in a wood-fired oven. Ciabatta is another good option.

Aged pecorino with raw sprouts, celery, and speck

This salad is all about combining ingredients with good compatible textures and flavors. It has a lovely clean taste. Serve on its own as an appetizer or with some peasant-style bread for a lunch.

Serves 4

6 Brussels sprouts

6$1/2$ ounces Pecorino Romano or Parmesan

2 or 3 celery stalks, washed

20 shelled hazelnuts

$1/2$ lemon

sea salt and freshly ground black pepper

$1/4$ cup extra virgin olive oil

12 slices of speck or prosciutto

small handful of curly parsley, leaves only, minced

Preheat the oven to 375°F (convection oven to 350°F). Wash the Brussels sprouts and pat dry. Using a small sharp knife, slice them as finely as you can and place in a bowl. Slice the cheese into fine shards. Add to the Brussels sprouts. Peel the celery with a swivel vegetable peeler to remove any stringy bits, then cut into shorter lengths and add to the bowl.

Scatter the hazelnuts on a baking sheet and warm in the oven until the nuts are lightly colored and release their flavor, 6 to 10 minutes. Let cool slightly, then rub in a cloth to remove the skins. Chop the nuts roughly and set aside.

Squeeze the lemon juice over the salad, season with salt and pepper to taste, and drizzle over three-quarters of the olive oil. Toss together lightly with your fingers.

Place a slice of speck on each plate and arrange half of the salad over it. Drape another slice of speck on top, then arrange the rest of the salad on top, finishing with a couple of slices of celery and a final slice of pecorino. Drizzle with the rest of the olive oil and scatter over the hazelnuts. Finish with a sprinkling of parsley.

When buying fresh porcini, look for caps that are firm and dry, not damp in any way. They should smell very fresh—a dank strong smell indicates that they are past their best. Don't keep mushrooms in plastic bags, as they will spoil very easily. Instead store them, loosely covered, in a basket—preferably in a cool pantry rather than the refrigerator, as cold can destroy their delicate flavor.

Wafer-thin slices of porcini with aged Parmesan and crème fraîche

Occasionally throughout this book, you will come across simple salads, comprising no more than two or three ingredients, served raw and finely sliced. It might seem surprising to eat mushrooms or asparagus uncooked, in their natural state, but cut as finely as possible, they often taste so much more of their true character to me. Cooking somehow seems to dilute their pure just-picked flavor. (Shown on pages 212-213.)

Serves 4

7 ounces porcini mushrooms
4¹/2 ounces aged Parmesan
¹/2 lemon
5 tsp mild-tasting good-quality extra virgin olive oil
sea salt and freshly ground black pepper
4 tbsp crème fraîche
handful of curly parsley, leaves only, minced

Wipe the mushrooms carefully and gently with a soft clean cloth or mushroom brush if you have one; don't wash them or the water will soak into the flesh and drown their flavor. Using a small sharp knife, trim the bases, then slice the porcini very finely into wafer-thin slices.

Slice the Parmesan very finely as well. To ensure that the Parmesan does not overpower the perfumed earthy, delicate flavor of the mushrooms, the slices need to be paper-thin.

Toss the sliced porcini and Parmesan together very gently, squeeze over the lemon juice, and drizzle with a little of the extra virgin olive oil. Season lightly with salt and pepper—these flavors are too delicate for enthusiastic seasoning. The salad is a whisper of flavors, no more.

Arrange the salad on individual plates, with a spoonful of crème fraîche in the center. Drizzle over the rest of the olive oil and sprinkle with parsley to serve.

Salad of warm torn bread, poached egg, and Parmesan dressing

I love a really good Caesar salad—it just seems hard to find one. This salad—of warm, plump poached fresh eggs; tasty salad leaves; a salty, creamy rich vinaigrette; and toast—isn't a Caesar, but its creation came about from a longing for similar flavors. It makes a great brunch or light lunch dish. I vary the leaves and sometimes add slivers of white celery heart. It is the dressing I am most drawn to though… and the bread with which to mop it up.

Serves 4

12 to 16 little plum tomatoes

sea salt and freshly ground black pepper

1/4 cup mild-tasting extra virgin olive oil

1 or 2 handfuls of mixed leaves, such as mustard leaf, arugula, or young spinach

4 slices of good-quality chewy, peasant-style bread, cut about 1/2 inch thick

1 clove garlic, peeled and halved

4 very fresh organic eggs

juice of 1/2 lemon

8 very thin slices of good-quality prosciutto

12 to 16 shards of Parmesan

Dressing

2 organic egg yolks

1 1/2 tsp English mustard powder

1 clove garlic, peeled

juice of 1 lemon

4 good-quality anchovy fillets in olive oil

2 1/4 ounces Parmesan, freshly grated

scant 2/3 cup mild-tasting extra virgin olive oil

1 tbsp crème fraîche

sea salt and freshly ground black pepper

Preheat the oven to 425°F (convection oven to 400°F). Pierce the tomatoes with a small knife just once and place on a baking sheet. Season with a little salt and pepper and drizzle with a little olive oil. Roast until the tomatoes are soft, 10 to 15 minutes. Remove and let cool, reserving the juices.

For the dressing, put the egg yolks, mustard, garlic, lemon juice, anchovies, and Parmesan into a blender. With the motor running, very slowly pour in the olive oil through the feeder tube. When all the oil is incorporated, you will have a creamy, slightly thick dressing. Add the crème fraîche and blend briefly to combine. Season generously with pepper, but only a little salt (you may not need any at all). The finished dressing should fall softly from a spoon. If it is too thick, stir in 1 tbsp or so of lukewarm water.

Place a wide pan of well-salted water on to boil. Wash the salad leaves and pat dry, then place in a bowl.

Preheat the broiler and toast the slices of bread until golden brown on both sides, then rub gently with the cut garlic clove. Brush the garlicky bread with a little olive oil and season with a little salt, then cut each slice in half.

Swirl the boiling water in the pan to create a whirlpool, then carefully break in the eggs and poach for 3 minutes. Meanwhile, lightly toss the salad leaves with the rest of the olive oil and the lemon juice, using your fingers. When the eggs are ready, remove and drain on paper towels.

To assemble, layer the salad, toast, prosciutto, Parmesan shards, and roasted tomatoes on warm individual plates, finishing with a piece of toast. Drizzle over the juice from the cooked tomatoes. Top with the poached egg and spoon over the dressing. Serve at once.

Scallops with arugula, fennel, toasted bread crumbs, and Dolcelatte dressing

This combination may seem a little strange, but the flavors are really quite lovely together. The contrast of broiled sweet, plump scallops and a creamy Dolcelatte dressing is seductive and sophisticated. Vary the leaves according to what is available—dandelion greens and young spinach also work well with these flavors.

Serves 4

20 sea scallops

1 small head of radicchio

handful of arugula leaves

1 fennel bulb

sea salt and freshly ground black pepper

finely grated zest of 1 lemon

juice of 1/2 lemon

4 tbsp extra virgin olive oil

handful of curly parsley, leaves only, minced

4 tbsp warm toasted sourdough bread crumbs (see opposite)

Dolcelatte dressing

1 organic egg yolk

3 1/4 ounces Dolcelatte

1 scant tbsp Dijon mustard

1 tbsp sherry vinegar

little squeeze of lemon juice

sea salt and freshly ground black pepper

1/2 cup mild-tasting virgin olive oil

1 tbsp crème fraîche

First make the dressing. Place the egg yolk, Dolcelatte, mustard, vinegar, and lemon juice in a blender. Add a small pinch of salt and a little pepper. Now turn on the motor and very slowly pour in the olive oil. Don't be tempted to add the oil too quickly, or the mixture may curdle. Once it's all been added, you should have a smooth, light brown sauce. Pour into a bowl, add the crème fraîche, and stir well to combine. Taste and adjust the seasoning if necessary; you are unlikely to need more salt.

Trim away the tough muscle from the side of each scallop. Set the scallops aside at room temperature while you prepare the salad.

Separate the radicchio leaves, wash gently, and pat dry using a clean dish towel. Do the same with the arugula. Remove the fibrous outer layer from the fennel, slice in half lengthwise, then cut into the finest long slices you can manage. Place the leaves and fennel in a bowl, season with a little salt and pepper, and add the lemon zest, lemon juice, and 3 tbsp of the olive oil. Toss together lightly with your fingers, taste for seasoning, and set aside.

Heat a large heavy skillet (preferably nonstick) over high heat. Season the scallops with salt and pepper and add the remaining 1 tbsp olive oil to the pan. When the skillet is very hot (starting to smoke), add the scallops, in a single layer. Cook without moving for 1 minute, then turn and cook for approximately 40 seconds on the other side. The scallops should have a crunchy exterior and the flesh inside should be sweet and soft. Remove from the heat.

Divide the dressed salad leaves among individual plates, arrange 5 scallops on top of each portion, and spoon over a little Dolcelatte dressing. Finish with a sprinkling of minced parsley and toasted bread crumbs. Serve at once—the scallops should be eaten as hot as possible.

Goat cheese soufflé with lemon thyme

I love the simplicity of cooking and serving a soufflé on a soup plate. I first ate a soufflé prepared in this way in a small restaurant in southwest France and was struck by its elegance. I like to serve it with a very simply dressed salad comprising only leaves. Sometimes there will be some good bread, too, but it doesn't really need it.

Serves 6

3 tbsp butter, melted

7 ounces Parmesan or romano, freshly grated

1 pound soft young lemony goat cheese (without rind)

7 organic eggs, separated

generous 2/3 cup heavy cream

small bunch of lemon thyme, leaves only

1 tsp minced dried red chile (optional)

sea salt and freshly ground black pepper

handful of warm toasted sourdough bread crumbs, to finish (optional)

Preheat the oven to 400°F (convection oven to 400°F). Brush six ovenproof soup plates with the melted butter and sprinkle with half of the Parmesan.

Crumble the goat cheese into a bowl, add the egg yolks and cream, and whisk until smooth. Add the lemon thyme and dried chile, then fold in the remaining Parmesan. Season with salt and pepper to taste.

Place the egg whites in a scrupulously clean bowl, add a pinch of salt, and whisk to firm peaks. Fold a third of the whisked whites into the cheese mixture until evenly incorporated, then carefully fold in the rest of the whites in two batches until thoroughly combined.

Divide the soufflé mixture among the soup plates. Set on a large baking sheet and place on the middle shelf of the oven. Bake until the soufflés are puffed and golden, 9 to 11 minutes. Remove from the oven, taking care as the plates will be very hot. Serve immediately, scattered with toasted bread crumbs for a contrast in texture.

For sourdough bread crumbs, whiz

chunks of sourdough bread in a food processor to rough bread crumbs. Tip into a bowl, season well, and toss with a good splash of olive oil. Scatter on a baking sheet and toast in the oven at 400°F (375°F for convection oven) for 12 to 15 minutes until golden and crunchy, shaking the sheet frequently to ensure they toast evenly.

Robiola with Malenca and pickled grapes

This is more a combination of very beautiful ingredients than a recipe. Robiola is a wonderfully luxurious triple milk cheese from Piedmont, Italy. It has a full, tangy flavor—slightly goaty, mushroomy, just a little citrusy, and sweet all at the same time. Malenca is a cured meat from the adjacent region of Lombardy, similar to bresaola, which is a suitable substitute. I like to slice it slightly thicker than bresaola, as it stands up better to the rich flavor of the robiola that way.

Serves 4

about 24 shelled hazelnuts (optional)

scant $1/3$ cup mild-tasting extra virgin olive oil

1 tbsp red wine vinegar

sea salt and freshly ground black pepper

3 celery stalks (from the sweet inner white heart)

handful or so of sweet young leaves, such as celery leaves, corn salad, or oak leaf

10 ounces robiola

12 slices of Malenca, bresaola, or prosciutto

20 pickled grapes or pickled cherries (page 29)

If using hazelnuts, preheat the oven to 425°F (convection oven to 400°F). Scatter the nuts on a baking sheet and toast until the skins begin to darken and split, 8 to 10 minutes. While still warm, scrunch them in a clean cloth to rub off most of their skins.

Whisk the olive oil and vinegar together with a pinch each of salt and pepper to make a dressing. Taste and adjust the seasoning.

Slice the celery on the diagonal. Wash and dry the salad leaves, place in a bowl, and add the celery. Toss lightly with the dressing.

Divide the salad among serving plates. Spoon the robiola on top, arrange the cured meat attractively around the cheese, and top with the pickled grapes. Scatter over the hazelnuts if using, and serve.

Manchego with quince paste

Quince, to me, is perhaps the most beautiful of all fruits. Heavy in size and pale green in color, it hangs so gracefully from its tree. I tend to make this rough paste every year, firstly because it is delicious and secondly because ritual is one of the nicest things about cooking with the seasons. I like to serve the quince paste with its classic partner manchego—preferably a slightly older cheese, as its sweet, chalky, crystally nature is just that much more intense.

Makes two 1-pound jars

Quince paste

12 quinces

2$1/4$ pounds sugar

To serve

about 2$1/4$ ounces manchego per serving

olive oil (optional)

Wipe the quinces with a clean damp cloth to remove the downy covering, then roughly chop the fruit. Place in a large nonreactive pan, add the sugar, then pour in enough water to just cover the fruit. Place over medium-low heat until the sugar has dissolved, then turn up the heat slightly and cook for 2$1/2$ hours, or until the fruit is a beautiful burned orange color and has completely fallen apart.

Remove from the heat, let cool slightly, then spoon the quince paste into sterilized jars. Store in the refrigerator or a cool dark pantry and use within 2 or 3 months. (You'll have enough here for plenty of cheese courses.)

To serve, slice the manchego and arrange on serving plates with a generous portion of quince paste. Everyone always tells me not to put olive oil on cheese, but I never listen—I think it's wonderful, so finish with a drizzle or two... if you approve.

Harder chalkier cheeses have a different taste when eaten thinly sliced, rather than in a thicker piece. It's nice to experience those differences, so try serving slices of varying thicknesses.

Honey

Over the past couple of years, I have become increasingly drawn to using honey in cooking. Sugar is one-dimensional in flavor, unless, of course, you play with it, taking it to a deep, rich caramel. By contrast, honey is complex and lends subtle flavor notes to dishes. Not only is it great to cook with, honey is also wonderful drizzled over cheeses, ice creams, and perfectly ripe seasonal fruit.

Honey is a natural product that very often sings of the terrain in which it was created. So, it is hardly surprising that there are almost as many varieties of honey as there are wines—each and every one with its very own distinctive flavor notes and character. Among my favorites are acacia, wildflower, and our locally produced honeys, but the one I love best of all is chestnut honey. The color of burned caramel—with a flavor to match—it is sublime drizzled over slivers of aged romano or Parmesan.

Honey is produced all over the world—from Siberia to the tropics. In warmer climates this can happen throughout the year, but in the very coldest countries the season can be as short as 2 or 3 weeks.

The type of flower from which the bee has collected the nectar determines a honey variety's distinct aroma, flavor, and color. And the resulting characteristics of the honey closely resemble the flavors of the flowers, trees, and herbs that the bees have visited.

Most honeys are what are known as polyfloral honeys, which means that the bees have taken nectar from many different floral sources. However, the most prized of all honeys are those from bees that have predominantly fed from the nectar of one plant species. These are known as monofloral. Of these, as I have said, chestnut honey is my favorite. Its flavor is so very particular that it can be quite shocking the first time you taste it. Not really sweet at all, the taste resonates to me of molasses, with a mildly bitter finish.

◊

Equally passionate about honey, my friend and mentor Wendy Fogarty summed it up perfectly when she said, "Honey tells us so much about the place it comes from. I love the fact that the complexity and majesty of nature can be so simply translated into this one single product."

Like vinegar, I usually have several different varieties of honey in my pantry, which I love to dip in and out of. There is light acacia honey that I have on sticky rye toast in the morning with cold unsalted butter. Sitting alongside is a jar of my favorite chestnut honey. And I always have some of our local honey—from nearby Richmond Park where it is produced in small quantites. Another fairly local honey I have to hand is from Brockwell Park in Brixton, produced by one man—Orlando Clarke. Urban honeys are not to be sniffed at, for they can be quite delicious.

◊

I find I use honey in all manner of dishes in the kitchen. Another of my breakfast favorites is toasted sourdough topped with young creamy goat cheese or ricotta and drizzled with honey.

A spoonful of honey stirred into warm oatmeal is delicious in the winter. During the warmer months, try soaking whole oats in freshly squeezed apple juice. Grate the flesh of an apple—skin and all—into the soaking oats and finish with a spoonful of honey. Cover and keep in the refrigerator overnight, then in the morning you will have a sweet, creamy breakfast cereal, known as Bircher muesli.

I also use honey in various dressings for salads and vegetables. At home, my daughter Evie is the queen of salad dressings. She often makes one my mother taught her, consisting of a teaspoon of honey, a little squeeze of orange juice, and a drop or two of soy sauce. This sweet, slightly salty dressing clings to the leaves irresistibly. I recommend that you try it.

Occasionally, I use honey to sweeten a creamy dressing. A little honey, a squeeze of lime, and perhaps a little minced fresh red chile stirred into crème fraîche or yogurt is delicious spooned over warm, roasted summer squash or pumpkin, for example.

In the fall, I'll often reach for a jar of honey when I'm making a salad dressing, as salads in the cooler months usually benefit from a slightly more robust dressing. A little honey mixed with Dijon mustard, sherry vinegar, and seasoning, and whisked with walnut oil makes for an interesting dressing, with all the right seasonal notes. Spoon it over a salad of tender roasted kabocha, young creamy walnuts, and fall salad leaves.

As for desserts, honey offers endless possibilities. Try adding a tablespoon or so to a chocolate sorbet or a chocolate truffle cake to lend a warm, sweet flavor, for instance.

When roasting fruit, I often substitute honey for sugar. It is delicious drizzled over sliced quince with some grated lemon zest and fresh bay, as indeed it is over pears, plums, medlars, or apricots.

And of course, if you are rounding off the meal with cheese and fruit, a drizzle of honey is often a perfect complement. There is no doubt that honey's complexity of flavor gives food a greater depth and often makes a dish taste more interesting.

Chicken with figs and honey

This dish, like so many, relies on using very good ingredients—lovely ripe figs and the best organic chicken that you can afford. It is unquestionably simple, but delicious. A salad of leaves dressed with nothing more than olive oil and lemon—and perhaps some good bread to mop up the juices—is all that is needed to accompany. (Shown on previous page.)

Serves 6

1 organic chicken, about 3¹/2 pounds, jointed into 6 to 8 pieces

sea salt and freshly ground black pepper

2 tbsp mild-tasting olive oil

1 medium yellow onion, peeled and sliced

few thyme sprigs

1 bay leaf

¹/2 cup medium-dry white wine

²/3 cup good-quality chicken stock

2 tbsp white wine vinegar

1 tbsp mild-tasting honey, such as acacia

10 ripe figs

Preheat the oven to 350°F (convection oven to 350°F). Trim off the excess fat from the chicken, then season it generously all over with salt and pepper.

Heat the olive oil in a large skillet over medium heat, then brown the seasoned chicken pieces in batches, skin side down, for about 8 minutes, turning to color them evenly all over. Remove the chicken to a Dutch oven or other heavy ovenproof pot with a slotted spoon. Pour off most of the fat from the skillet, then add the onion and cook over low heat for 5 minutes to soften.

Add the onion to the pot with the thyme and bay leaf. Pour over the wine and the stock. Place the pot, uncovered, on the middle shelf of the oven and cook until the meat is tender but not quite falling from the bone, 20 to 30 minutes. The skin should now be golden and the liquid reduced by about half.

Place the pot over low heat on the stove top. Mix the vinegar and honey together and pour in. Tear each of the ripe figs into four and add to the pot. Turn up the heat and bring to a boil. Let bubble until the liquor has reduced to a syrupy consistency—it should be glossy and taste both sweet and sour. Serve on warm plates, with a salad and some bread.

Honey in savory dishes can be delicious, but it must be counterbalanced with a certain amount of acidity to redress the balance. The Italians call this balance of sweet and sour *agrodolce*.

Baked Sauternes and honey custard

We first made this custard a couple of years ago, when Maggie Beer came to visit us at Petersham. A warm, vibrant bundle of energy, she is one of my favorite cooks—representing to me everything that's wonderful about cooking! This recipe is adapted from one in her lovely book, *Maggie's Orchard*. We serve this custard with roasted rhubarb during the late winter and early spring months.

Serves 6

1 1/2 cups Sauternes

2 cups heavy cream

1/2 vanilla bean, split lengthwise

1/2 cup superfine sugar

2 tbsp honey (rhododendron, or any other monofloral honey with a pronounced flavor)

7 organic egg yolks

Preheat the oven to 350°F (convection oven to 350°F). Pour the wine into a heavy pan and bring to a boil over medium heat. Let bubble until reduced by half, then remove from the heat.

In a separate pan, slowly warm the cream with the vanilla bean, then stir into the reduced wine.

In a large bowl, beat the sugar and honey together to combine, then incorporate the egg yolks one at a time, beating well after each addition. Pour on the wine and cream mixture, stirring well with a whisk as you do so.

Pour the mixture into a shallow ovenproof dish, measuring about 10 by 6 inches, and place the dish in a roasting pan containing enough hot water to come halfway up the side of the dish. Place on the middle shelf of the oven and bake until the custard is set but still quite wobbly in the center, 40 to 45 minutes.

Let cool to room temperature before serving. The custard is also wonderfully refreshing served chilled on a hot day.

Baked pears with honey, Marsala, and bay

This is a beautiful, uncomplicated dessert for fall or early winter. Serve it warm, not hot, with a generous spoonful of crème fraîche or good homemade vanilla ice cream (see page 34). I generally allow one pear per person, but you might like to bake a few extra and put them in the middle of the table for guests to help themselves to an extra half pear.

Serves 6 to 8

8 firm ripe pears, such as Comice or Bosc

2¹/2 cups Marsala

scant 1 cup fragrant honey, such as rhododendron or a mountain or forest honey

1 cinnamon stick

1 vanilla bean, split lengthwise

finely grated zest of 1 lemon

sprig of bay leaves (4 or 5 leaves)

Preheat the oven to 425°F (convection oven to 400°F). Place the pears in a roasting dish in which they fit quite snugly, with their stalks uppermost. Pour over the Marsala and drizzle over the honey, then add the cinnamon stick, vanilla bean, lemon zest, and bay leaves. Cover the dish tightly with foil.

Place the roasting dish on the middle shelf of the oven and roast for 15 to 20 minutes. Remove the foil and bake, uncovered, until the pears are soft and the skin slightly wrinkly, 15 to 20 minutes. Let cool to room temperature.

Serve the pears on individual plates with the Marsala and honey syrup spooned over.

Chocolate

There is an aura of luxury about chocolate—it feels indulgent, almost clandestine. We make a decision to eat chocolate in a way that we don't make about eating other food ... a considered "Shall I?" and if the answer is "Yes," we are likely to feel slightly decadent about our decision. Each little mouthful is savored, sometimes with an association of guilt. Yet above all, chocolate is treasured— a gift for loved ones on special occasions. Somehow it gives a message to the recipient that they are valued and special—and therefore so is chocolate itself.

When it comes to cooking, I recommend that you buy the finest quality chocolate you can afford—dark purple-black in color, glossy, and bitter, with an almost smoky quality. In my view, chocolate desserts should be intensely rich, but not too sweet—and eaten in small quantities for ultimate pleasure.

For centuries, chocolate has been prized around the world. It is produced, of course, from the beans of the cacao tree (*Theobroma cacao*) native to South America; *Theobroma* meaning "food of the gods." As long as 3,500 years ago chocolate was produced in Mexico, though right up until the 1800s it was only ever consumed in the form of a drink; in fact, the word chocolate means "hot beverage."

Chocolate as we know it today is made from the seeds (or beans) of the cacao pods. The beans are fermented, dried, roasted, and hulled in order to separate the nibs from their shells. The nibs are then ground and melted to make a paste known as chocolate liquor. On cooling, this sets and hardens to become unsweetened cooking chocolate. At this stage, it consists of nothing more than half cocoa butter and half cocoa solids. Other things are later mixed in, such as sugar, vanilla, and milk; in lesser quality products, emulsifiers and stabilizers are often added, too.

The chocolate is now "conched" (or kneaded) for at least 12 hours (as long as 3 days for fine-quality chocolate) to make it as smooth as possible and eliminate any gritty texture. Finally it is "tempered" or cooled and reheated in several controlled stages so that it hardens to a shiny gloss and snaps when broken. The chocolate is then aged for 60 to 90 days.

You may have heard of couverture in connection with chocolate for cooking. This is chocolate with a high cocoa-butter content, designed to provide a thin even coating and a high finished gloss. It is also good for more general use, due to its superior quality.

◊

At the restaurant, we use the best quality chocolate that we can find, usually Valrhona, an intense and beautiful chocolate from France (64 percent cocoa solids minimum), or Amedei, an Italian chocolate made by a family in Tuscany.

Dark chocolate has a shelf life of about a year. It is best kept in a cool pantry or drawer—in one large block rather than pieces and wrapped in foil. Storing chocolate at a higher temperature can cause cocoa butter to rise to the surface causing dull brown patches known as a "bloom" to appear, making the chocolate unusable. Conversely, if you keep chocolate in the refrigerator, the humidity can cause white "sugar bloom" spots to form on the surface.

◊

Melting chocolate The best way to melt chocolate is in a double boiler or a heatproof bowl set over a pan of gently simmering water. It is important that the bowl in which the chocolate is to melt does not sit directly in the water. Break up or chop the chocolate first to

Rich and intensely flavored, good-quality chocolate should be eaten in small pieces. Don't rush it—let it linger in your mouth and savor its lovely bitter, smoky aroma and flavor. Like many good things, a little goes a long way.

encourage it to melt evenly and don't stir it during melting as this can dull the shine. If you are melting chocolate with cream, then you can stir the pieces of chocolate directly into the hot cream; otherwise, add chocolate to cool liquids rather than hot and melt slowly and gently in a pan over direct heat.

◊

When it comes to pairing chocolate with other flavors, dark, salty caramels; almonds; hazelnuts; coffee; and candied citrus fruit work best. With the exception of citrus fruits and a few others, I find fresh fruits less compatible with chocolate. Slightly bitter oranges complement dark chocolate beautifully; cherries and chocolate are also natural partners. And if a chocolate dessert calls for some cream on the side, I'll invariably serve it with a bowl of thick unpasteurized cream as opposed to crème fraîche, whose slightly sharp acidity tends to rub against the smooth flavor of the chocolate rather than enhance it.

Hazelnuts go particularly well with chocolate, providing a texture and flavor that are truly compatible. Their earthy flavor serves to balance the rich bitterness of good-quality dark chocolate.

Chocolate mousse

Perfecting a chocolate mousse seemed to take us forever. I was looking for a mousse that was rich, yet very definitely light, with a certain density about it. Also, I wanted to serve it freeform on a plate, but to do that the flavor had to be elegant ... even smoky. This is what we finally came up with, thanks largely to the work of Sophie Cookes, who was with us in the kitchen at the time. It needs to be served with something to counterbalance its intensity. Here I've chosen my favorite accompaniment—salty, almost burned, caramel ... and cream, of course.

Serves 8

10^1/2 ounces good-quality dark chocolate (minimum 64% cocoa solids), in pieces

8 organic eggs, separated

^{1}/2 cup superfine sugar

pinch of sea salt

Salty caramel

1^1/4 cups superfine sugar

13/4 cups water

generous pinch of sea salt

Take this salty caramel as far as you dare. It calls for a little courage but I take it to where I can just smell the burn. Visually, I love a rich, dark caramel; one that is too pale looks—and tastes—insipid. This is a good example of all our senses playing a role in our cooking—sight, sound, smell, and, of course, taste.

Melt the chocolate slowly in a heatproof bowl set over a pan of gently simmering water (see page 236), then remove from the heat and let cool slightly. Meanwhile, beat the egg yolks and half the sugar together in a bowl until pale and thick. Slowly incorporate the melted chocolate.

In a clean bowl, whisk the egg whites with the salt until soft peaks form, then gradually whisk in the remaining sugar. Carefully fold the egg whites into the chocolate mixture, a third at a time, until evenly combined. Pour into a large bowl, cover, and place in the refrigerator to set.

For the salty caramel, place the sugar and ^{1}/2 cup water in a small heavy pan over very low heat and, without stirring, let the sugar dissolve. Once dissolved, turn up the heat to fairly high and bring to a boil. Cook until the caramel begins to color; this will take at least 5 minutes. When it starts to brown around the sides, watch it carefully—as it will then darken quite quickly.

Once the caramel has reached a deep mahogany color, quickly and carefully pour in the remaining 1^1/4 cups water. Cook, stirring, for another 2 minutes to loosen the caramel and ensure that it doesn't set hard. Finally, throw in the salt, stir once or twice, then remove from the heat. Pour into a heatproof bowl and let cool, then let chill.

To serve, spoon the chocolate mousse onto plates and serve with the salty caramel and cream.

Rich chocolate ice cream

I love ice cream—primarily because I really enjoy making it, which we do almost every day of the year at the restaurant. More often than not, our ices are fruit based but occasionally we make this chocolate ice cream. It took quite a few attempts to get it right because I wanted something very rich and luxurious, yet a custard base will only take so much chocolate before it refuses to freeze.

Serves 4 to 6

2/3 cup whole milk

1 1/2 cups heavy cream

1 vanilla bean, split lengthwise

2 1/4 ounces good-quality dark chocolate (minimum 64% cocoa solids)

6 organic egg yolks

2/3 cup superfine sugar

2 tbsp unsweetened cocoa

Pour the milk and cream into a heavy pan, add the vanilla bean, place over medium heat, and bring to a boil. Chop the chocolate into rough chunks, add to the hot creamy milk, and stir once or twice to encourage it to melt.

While the chocolate is melting, beat the egg yolks and sugar together in a bowl for a minute or so until thick and pale. Sift the cocoa over the surface and stir to combine. Pour on the hot cream, whisking as you do so, then pour back into the pan.

Turn the heat to very low and stir, using a figure eight motion, until the custard thickens. You'll need to be patient as this will take 8 to 10 minutes. Don't be tempted to rush the process by turning up the heat as it may cause the custard to curdle. As soon as the custard is thick enough to lightly coat the back of a wooden spoon, remove from the heat and strain through a fine strainer into a bowl.

Let cool completely, then pour the custard into your ice-cream maker and churn until thickened. When it is ready, freeze in a suitable container. The ice cream will be ready to eat in a couple of hours and will keep well for a day or so, but no longer. Homemade ice cream is better eaten relatively soon after it has been made. Spoon into chilled bowls to serve.

Zuppa inglese

In many ways, this Italian version of an English trifle is a departure from the desserts we usually make in the restaurant. The inspiration for it comes from a recipe written by Mario Batalli, who is a fine chef and food writer. Rich, creamy, and indulgent, with just enough orange syrup and lemon zest added to make it light—it has a cheekiness about it that I find endearing. (Shown on previous page.)

Serves 8

2¹/2 cups whole milk

grated zest of 2 oranges

grated zest of 1 lemon

1 vanilla bean, split lengthwise

8 organic eggs

²/3 cup superfine sugar

scant 1 cup all-purpose flour

5 tbsp good-quality unsweetened cocoa

3¹/4 ounces good-quality dark chocolate (minimum 64% cocoa solids), chopped

scant ¹/3 cup limoncello

20 ladyfingers (Italian savoiardi)

Candied oranges

2 oranges

1¹/4 cups superfine sugar

generous 1 cup water

First prepare the candied oranges. Slice the oranges into fine circles and blanch in a pan of boiling water for 1 minute or so. Drain and refresh in cold water. Repeat this blanching process twice more. Dissolve the sugar in the water in a small heavy pan over medium heat, then bring to a boil. Add the oranges, turn down the heat slightly, and cook for 10 to 15 minutes, or until the syrup is viscous and the oranges are translucent. Remove from the heat and set aside to cool.

Pour the milk into a heavy pan and add the orange and lemon zests. Scrape the seeds from the vanilla bean and add to the pan with the empty bean. Heat to a simmer, then immediately remove from the heat and set aside to infuse for 15 minutes.

Put the eggs, sugar, and flour into a large bowl and whisk, using an electric beater, until the mixture is pale and thick. Slowly pour on the milk, whisking as you do so. Pour back into the pan and whisk over low heat until the custard thickens enough to coat the back of a wooden spoon and no longer tastes floury. Immediately pour into two bowls, dividing it equally and discarding the vanilla bean. Add the cocoa and chocolate to one bowl and stir until the cocoa is evenly distributed and the chocolate has melted. Set the bowls of vanilla and chocolate custard aside to cool.

Drain the oranges, reserving the syrup, and chop into small pieces. Stir the limoncello into the syrup. Take a tablespoon of the syrup and stir it into the vanilla custard. Split the ladyfingers in half lengthwise and sprinkle with the remaining orange syrup.

Arrange a layer of the soaked ladyfingers over the bottom of a pretty serving bowl. Top with a layer of vanilla custard, then a scattering of chopped orange. Add another layer of ladyfingers, followed by chocolate custard, then orange. Continue in this way until you've used all the ingredients, finishing with a few spoonfuls each of the vanilla and chocolate custards. Swirl together to create a marbled effect, then refrigerate for at least an hour before serving.

Warm chocolate puddings

These comforting little treats literally ooze chocolate from their center. Gooey and molten, they are wonderful served simply with cream. I also like them with coffee ice cream or cream flavored with a touch of honey.

Serves 6

1/2 cup plus 2 tbsp unsalted butter, plus extra to grease

10 ounces good-quality dark chocolate (minimum 64% cocoa solids)

4 organic eggs

3 organic egg yolks

3/4 cup superfine sugar

1/3 cup all-purpose flour

Lightly butter 6 individual ovenproof ramekins or custard cups, 7-ounce capacity. Using a sharp knife, chop the chocolate into 3/4-inch chunks. Melt the chocolate and butter together in a heatproof bowl set over a pan of gently simmering water (see page 236), then remove from the heat and let cool slightly.

Meanwhile, using an electric mixer, beat together the whole eggs, egg yolks, and sugar until pale and mousselike. This will take about 5 minutes—the beaters should leave a ribbonlike trail on the surface of the mixture as you lift them.

Gently and carefully pour in the chocolate, folding it in lightly but thoroughly to combine. Sift the flour from a good height over the surface and fold in carefully. Spoon the mixture into the prepared molds and place in the refrigerator for an hour.

Preheat the oven to 400°F (convection oven to 400°F). Stand the molds on a baking sheet and bake in the oven until the puddings are puffed up with a slight crust, 16 to 18 minutes. Turn out onto warm plates and serve immediately ... they will smell and taste delicious!

Less is more with food, especially desserts like this. To my mind, your last mouthful should leave you wanting perhaps just one more spoonful. Food should linger as a lovely memory— a thought, a dream.

Chocolate panna cotta with warm berries and honey

Rich, creamy, and a little wobbly, this dessert needs to be served cool from the refrigerator—ideally within 24 hours, as the gelatin continues to set the mixture as long as it sits in the refrigerator. Blackberries in warm honey go beautifully, but you can serve it just as it is, or with salty caramel (see page 239). Ripe strawberries and cream would be the perfect accompaniment in summer.

Serves 4

a little oil, for the molds

7 ounces good-quality dark chocolate (minimum 64% cocoa solids)

3 sheets of leaf gelatin

generous 3/4 cup whole milk

generous 1 cup heavy cream

1/2 cup superfine sugar

1 vanilla bean, split lengthwise

Blackberries and honey

generous 3/4 cup honey (I like to use chestnut honey or lighter acacia honey)

1 1/3 cups blackberries

Lightly oil 4 individual panna cotta molds or other individual ovenproof bowls, 7-ounce capacity.

Chop the chocolate into small pieces and melt slowly, without stirring, in a heatproof bowl set over a pan of gently simmering water (see page 236). Remove from the heat and set aside to cool slightly. Soak the gelatin leaves in cold water to cover for about 5 minutes to soften.

In the meantime, put the milk, cream, and sugar into a heavy pan. Scrape the seeds from the vanilla bean and add these to the pan with the empty bean. Place over medium heat and bring to a gentle simmer, stirring once or twice to help dissolve the sugar. Remove from the heat and strain through a fine strainer onto the melted chocolate, stirring well to combine.

If necessary, return the chocolate mixture to the pan and reheat gently—it needs to be very hot but not quite boiling. Remove from the heat. Squeeze the gelatin to remove excess water and add to the chocolate mixture, stirring to dissolve.

Strain the mixture through a fine strainer into a pitcher, then pour into the prepared molds. Let cool completely, then refrigerate for at least 2 hours before serving.

For the accompanying berries, warm the honey in a small pan. Add two-thirds of the blackberries and cook gently until they have begun to bleed into the warm honey. Remove from the heat and stir in the remaining blackberries.

To serve, quickly dip the base of each mold into hot water to loosen the base and sides, then run a small sharp knife around the top and invert the panna cotta onto a plate. Spoon the warm blackberries and honey over the panna cottas and serve, with a bowl of rich yellow cream on the side if you like.

Chocolate and hazelnut cake

I like to take this cake from the oven when it is still very wobbly in the center. It oozes a little when you cut into it—the soft, fluid dense chocolate in the middle is my favorite bit, eaten with a spoonful of rich, thick buttercup yellow cream. It is delicious warm or cold. You can even keep it in the refrigerator for a couple of days—the texture will be firmer in the center, but it still tastes good.

Serves 8 to 10

generous 1 1/2 cups unsalted butter, plus extra to grease

1/2 cup all-purpose flour, plus extra to dust

scant 1/2 cup shelled hazelnuts

13 ounces good-quality dark chocolate (minimum 64% cocoa solids)

9 organic eggs, separated

1 1/2 cups superfine sugar

pinch of sea salt

confectioners' sugar, to dust

Preheat the oven to 365°F (convection oven to 340°F). Butter and flour a 10 1/2-inch round cake pan. Spread the hazelnuts out on a baking sheet and put them in the warm oven for 2 to 4 minutes, just to tickle out their flavor. Let cool slightly, then rub in a cloth to remove the skins. Grind the nuts, using a mortar and pestle or blender, leaving the texture slightly uneven—this makes for a more interesting cake.

Chop both the chocolate and the butter into small chunks and place in a heatproof bowl set over a pan of gently simmering water to melt (see page 236). Don't stir until the very end; just let them melt together slowly. Once melted, stir once or twice to combine and remove from the heat. Let cool slightly.

Meanwhile, beat the egg yolks and sugar together in a bowl until pale and thick. Pour in the melted chocolate and stir gently to combine. Sift the flour over the surface and add the ground nuts. Fold in lightly until evenly combined.

Place the egg whites in a very clean bowl with the salt. Whisk, slowly to begin with until the whites have broken down, then more quickly until soft peaks form. Carefully fold into the chocolate mixture and pour into the prepared cake pan.

Bake on the middle shelf of the oven for 40 to 50 minutes, or until just set, but still wobbly in the center. Leave in the pan for 10 minutes, then turn out and place on a wire rack to cool. Serve warm or cold, dusted with confectioners' sugar.

Index

Acknowledgments

Thank you first and foremost to my children, Holly and Evie, who let me go to work and do the thing that I love, even though I think they would prefer for me to stay at home.
A special thanks to all those I work with every day, for they make my working life such a joy. Thank you to Jason Lowe for his beautiful photographs. It is always a joy to work with him, as it is to work with my editor, Janet Illsley, and designer Lawrence Morton. Thank you also to publishing director Jane O'Shea, and to everyone at Quadrille Publishing.

Text copyright ©2010, 2008
by Skye Gyngell
Photographs copyright © 2008
by Jason Lowe
Design and layout copyright ©
2008 by Quadrille Publishing
Limited

All rights reserved.

Published in the United States
by Ten Speed Press,
an imprint of the Crown Publishing
Group, a division of Random House,
Inc., New York.
www.crownpublishing.com
www.tenspeed.com

Ten Speed Press and the Ten Speed
Press colophon are registered
trademarks of Random House, Inc.

Originally published in hardcover
in Great Britain in 2008.

Library of Congress
Cataloging-in-Publication Data

Gyngell, Skye.
My favorite ingredients : an enticing
collection of recipes / Skye Gyngell; -
photography by Jason Lowe.
      p. cm.
Originally published: London :
Quadrille Publishing Ltd.
Includes index.
Summary: "A celebrated UK chef
shares her sixteen best-loved
ingredients and demonstrates how
to combine them with a wide range
of fresh foods in this collection of
100 seasonal recipes"—Provided by
publisher.
1. Cookery. 2. Petersham Nurseries
Café. I. Title.
TX714.G895 2010
641.5—dc22

2009032641

ISBN: 978-1-58008-050-7

Printed in China

Editorial director
Jane O'Shea

Creative director
Helen Lewis

Project editor
Janet Illsley

Art direction & design
Lawrence Morton

Photographer
Jason Lowe

Stylist
Cynthia Inions

Production director
Vincent Smith

Production controller
Marina Asenjo

3 1901 04485 5973